ECUMENICAL JIHAD

PETER KREEFT

ECUMENICAL JIHAD

Ecumenism and the Culture War

IGNATIUS PRESS   SAN FRANCISCO

Chapter 7, "Is There Such a Thing as 'Mere Christianity'?:
A Trialogue with C. S. Lewis, Martin Luther, and Thomas Aquinas",
has been adapted from an article published in
New Oxford Review: July–August, 1994.
Copyright © 1994, *New Oxford Review*.
Adapted with permission from
New Oxford Review, 1069 Kains Avenue, Berkeley, CA 94706.

Cover design by Roxanne Mei Lum
Cover art:
School of Novgorod
St. George and the Dragon (detail)
Russian State Museum, St. Petersburg, Russia
Scala/Art Resource, NY

For
Chuck Colson,
Michael Medved,
and
Richard John Neuhaus

fellow footsoldiers
wielding pens
mightier than swords

CONTENTS

INTRODUCTION

What a strange title! How unusual a juxtaposition: bringing together the two ideas of ecumenism and "jihad".

Twentieth-century minds still react that way. To the twenty-first century, the juxtaposition will appear not at all strange but obvious. It's an idea that, once you see it, makes you shake your head and say: "How could I have missed it for so long?"

Old categories often obscure. The categories "liberal" and "conservative" are such categories: once useful in politics, perhaps still useful there (or perhaps not), but certainly not useful in religion or culture. Ecumenism is a "liberal" idea and one that makes "conservatives" suspicious. "Jihad" is a "conservative" idea and one that makes "liberals" suspicious. Bringing these two ideas together in this book will probably make both sides suspicious. Good. I will teach something to offend everybody—just as my heroes Jesus and Socrates did.

One of the main points of this book is that we need to change our current categories and our current alignments. We need to realize, first, that we are at war and, second, that the sides have changed radically: many of our former enemies (for example, Muslims) are now our friends, and some of our former friends (for example, humanists) are now our enemies.

You don't have to agree with this contention to read the book. I don't assume it or declare it dogmatically; I try to show it. You can't afford not to look, because, if there's even a chance that it's true, or half-true, it changes everything, like sunrise on a battlefield.

* * *

The main point is put in the first chapter, "Ecumenical Jihad".

Two converging lines of evidence then stem from, or lead to, that main point: one about jihad and the other about ecumenism.

Chapters 2 to 4 are about the "culture war". They defend the concept of spiritual warfare. "Liberals" who sail near the shores of secular humanism will get the willies from these chapters.

Chapters 5 to 8 defend the concept of ecumenism. "Conservatives" who sail near the shores of Fundamentalism will get the willies from these chapters.

That's because both are still living in the past. This book is a wake-up call.

Chapter One

Ecumenical Jihad

The Problem: "Today" = "Decay"

Picture to yourself the scene. You are Augustine, and you have just heard the news: the unthinkable has happened. Rome, the Eternal City, the heart of the world's first and only unified global civilization, has fallen. The brink of a long Dark Age is opening up before your feet. What do you do?

You do one of the most radical things a man can do: you write a book—the world's first philosophy of history, *The City of God*, a book that would be a lantern for millions through the darkly twisting roads of history for the rest of time, a book that demands to be dusted off and reread almost sixteen centuries later, now that another and far more formidable Dark Age looms ahead: not the Age of the Barbarians, but the Age of the Antichrist.

As Augustine lay dying in North Africa, he could see the fires of his burning city, an echo of Rome's fall. When the queen bee falls, the other bees in the hive cannot survive. Rome was the queen bee then; America is the world's queen bee today. Our empire is cultural, not military, but most of the world is becoming increasingly Americanized. What happens here happens everywhere. And what is happening here is very clear. Increasingly, "Americanized" is coming to mean "adulterated, sodomized, contracepted, aborted, and euthanized". Pious Muslims call us "the great Satan" and see us as a necrotic tumor in the body of humanity.

What we are seeing happening here with increasing clarity is exactly that spiritual war between "the City of God" and "the City of the World" that Augustine detected as the fundamental plot of human history. For the first time in the history of America, the term "culture war" is now becoming familiar and accepted.

The war is very old, of course—as old as Eden. What is new is the global strategy of the City of the World. It is more and more coming out of hiding. The battle lines are becoming clearer. The war on earth is more closely resembling the war in Heaven. Time is more closely mirroring eternity, as if Platonic archetypes were incarnating themselves, inhabiting their earthly instances, like ghosts haunting houses.

At Armageddon there will be no more uncertainty, no neutral corners. Armageddon is approaching. It may be a million years away—or a dozen—but it is approaching, like a wave from the invisible other side of the world. If you listen, you can almost hear the sound of millions of troops being moved, like cosmic chess pieces, jostling for position, spirit-wings opening and closing.

This is not fantasy or mythology. The spiritual war is literal. It is fully as real as any physical war. It has real casualties: eternal souls. It also has physical casualties that already surpass in number those of any war in history. In America alone, the blood of thirty million unborn babies has been spilled into the thirsty maw of Moloch.

Why now? Why so suddenly? A modern Rip Van Winkle falling asleep in 1955 and waking up in 1995 would simply not believe his ears when he heard the statistics of our decay. What moralist, complaining of the 10-percent divorce rate then, foresaw the 50-percent divorce rate now? Who foresaw a 500-percent increase in violent crime and a *5000-percent* increase in teenage violent crime? When Black society was being declared beyond repair because of a 30-percent illegitimacy rate, who thought that by 1995 white society would equal it, while the rate would climb to nearly 80 percent among Blacks? Who would have thought even ten years ago that Russian public schools would be showing films about Jesus and American schools would be outlawing them? If the next forty years continue the movement of the last forty, does anyone have the slightest hope for the survival of anything resembling civilization? What would another 5000-percent increase in teenage violent crime mean? Or another tripling of the illegitimacy rate? Or another administration that would be to the Clinton what the Clinton was to the Eisenhower, one that would make the Clinton years look like Ozzie and Harriet? Just extend the line, follow the road, and you will see the cliff.

Many of our citizens simply have not heard the statistics of decay, though they live them; and most of those who know the symptoms do not know the disease that is causing them. They wonder what the source is of the massive destruction of morality and safety and families and marriages and trust and the sanctity of life and sex, and even belief in objective truth and goodness—all these things at once! The root cause of all these poisonous fruits is not obvious, because it is invisible. It is spiritual, not political or economic or military or criminological. No such partial cause can account for such a massive darkness descending over everything at once, like the night sky, spread over the whole world like an eclipse of the sun, or an eclipse of the Son of God.

As the City of the World increasingly oozes its decay, what of the City of God? What is "the City set on a hill" doing about the fact that all the septic tanks below are backing up?

It is riddled with division and dissent: division between Eastern and Western religions, division in the West among Jew, Christian, and Muslim, division within Christendom among Protestant, Catholic, and Orthodox, and division within Protestantism among some two thousand (or, according to some estimates, as many as twenty thousand) Protestant denominations. (Perhaps some of these twenty thousand denominations contain only one member?) The Enemy's battle strategy has been the oldest and most obvious in military science: divide and conquer. Insofar as he has been able to foment civil wars and divide God's people, he has been able to weaken them.

And he has fomented wars not only *between* churches but also *within* them. Within the Roman Catholic Church in the United States, middle management is dominated by the "dissenters". (They used to be called "heretics". People who call moral *laws* "values" also call heretics "dissenters".) These "dissenters", or "cafeteria Catholics", now control nearly all major Catholic university theology departments, ensuring that the majority of freshmen who enter with a robust faith will graduate as seniors with a mushy one or none at all. Already a generation ago Archbishop Fulton Sheen was telling Catholic parents: "The best way I know to be sure that your children will lose their faith is to send them to Catholic colleges."

What is this dissent about? Are the Nestorian or Docetistic or Apollinarian or Monophysite heresies being revived? No, the dissent is almost always moral. And within moral theology, do the dissenters defend theft or rape or oppression or nuclear war or slavery? No. Within the moral area, the dissent is almost always about one thing: sex. Every one of the hot topics today, each of the controversial issues about which dissenters dissent from the Church, concerns traditional sexual morality versus the sexual revolution, which the Church stubbornly refuses to bless. Abortion, contraception, fornication, adultery, divorce, homosexual acts, priestesses, even "inclusive language"—all sexual issues.

Even theological controversies like the dating of the Gospels are often driven by sexual motors. The connecting chain is clear. If the Gospels were not written by contemporary eyewitnesses and do not tell us the words of God incarnate but only the words of man, or (as the favorite code word goes) "the early Christian community", then their authority, and that of the Church they say Christ founded, is undermined. Authority over what? Guess. The biblical Modernist's "historical-critical" strategy is often driven by the demand somehow to break one of the links of the iron chain that binds our gonads to our God.

There is a silly saying that "the way to a man's heart is through his stomach." Satan has used sounder psychology: the way to a man's heart is through his hormones. This was the philosophy echoed on the sign on Chuck Colson's desk when he was working for Nixon instead of for God: "When you got them by their balls, their hearts and minds will follow."

Satan has pursued a Spectacularly Successful Seven-Step Sexual Strategy:

Step 1: The *summum bonum*, the ultimate end, is to win souls.

Step 2: A powerful means to this end is the corruption of society. This works especially well in a society of conformists, of other-directed people. After all, a good society is simply one that makes it easy to be good, to use Peter Maurin's words. The satanic corollary is also true: a bad society makes it easy to be bad. Has there ever been a time when we have had more and easier opportunities to be bad?

Step 3: The most powerful means to destroy society is to destroy its one absolutely fundamental building block, the family, the only institution where most of us learn life's most important lesson, unselfish love.

Step 4: The family is destroyed by destroying its foundation, stable marriage.

Step 5: Marriage is destroyed by loosening its glue, sexual fidelity.

Step 6: Fidelity is destroyed by the sexual revolution.

Step 7: And the sexual revolution is propagated mainly by the media, which are now massively in enemy hands.

The sexual revolution will quite possibly prove to be the most destructive revolution in history, far more than any political or military revolution, because it touches not only *lives* but the very wellsprings of *life*. It is still in its infancy. We are only halfway to *Brave New World*. We do not yet see all of the consequences of moral relativism. At present, other areas of morality are not yet massively revolutionized in practice, as sex has been. This can only be temporary. Once Satan's soldiers secure this part of the battlefield, they will begin to attack the next one. Already, the governments in Holland and Oregon say it's OK to kill people to save them from pain. The same hedonism fuels the euthanasia movement as fuels the sexual revolution: it is the un-Socratic principle that "the unpleasant life is not worth living."

The most dramatic triumph of the sexual revolution, the Dunkirk of its enemies, has surely been the enthronement of abortion. If there is any one principle of morality that one may think so obvious that it could never be eradicated from the human heart, it is surely: Thou Shalt Not Murder (that is, kill innocent human beings). Yet the sexual revolution has already conquered conscience's surprisingly vulnerable hold on this principle; for abortion means the willingness to murder for the sake of the willingness to copulate. Pro-choicers are repeatedly telling me that the abortion battle is not over babies but over sex. It makes sense. Think about it. If abortion had nothing to do with sex, it would never have been legalized. Why does anyone want an abortion? Abortion is demanded as a form of birth control, backup birth control. And why is birth control demanded? Birth control is the demand to have sex without having babies. If storks brought babies, Wade would have defeated Roe. Most sins against the Fifth Commandment stem from sins against the Sixth. More than 99 percent of all murders in the United States are abortions.

We are even willing to *murder* to preserve our so-called sexual freedom. And we will murder *the most innocent* among us, the only innocent among us. And *the most defenseless* of all. And in the teeth of *the strongest instinct*: motherhood. It is a miracle of black magic, a stunning success, explainable only by supernatural power and defeatable only by supernatural power. Argument is insufficient; America needs exorcism.

The *Only* Solution to the Crisis

There are not a number of possible solutions to this problem. There is only one. It has two parts.

Unless two principles are as certain in our minds as they are in fact, we will continue to treat this cancer with aspirin, and our society will die, as Rome did, whether with a bang or with a whimper.

> First principle: The foundation of social order is morality.
> Second principle: The foundation of morality is religion.

1. No society has ever succeeded without morality. As everyone knows, moral *practice* in America is declining at an alarmingly rapid rate. But not everyone knows that the decline of moral *principles*—objective moral laws as distinct from subjective personal values—is even more radical and more destructive. For a nation that does not practice its principles can at least still *have* principles and can therefore be recalled to them. If the road maps are still there, we can find

our way back to the road. But to disbelieve in principles is to burn the maps; and how likely is it then that we will find our way back?

Here is just a tiny sample of the evidence that the map-burning is in a very advanced state, two typical facts out of thousands:

a. Not one nonreligious law school in America teaches, or even, usually, tolerates, the theory of a real Natural Moral Law. Remember how terrified Clarence Thomas' senatorial inquisitors were at his having written a few nice things about the Natural Law? How awful! A potential Supreme Court Justice who actually believes in real Justice!

b. In a nationwide poll a few years ago, only 11 percent of future teachers in schools of education said that among the different options they could in good conscience present to their students as alternative moral theories was the belief that there was a real, objective, absolute morality. Eighty-nine percent of our children's future teachers said that this idea was not one they could even *tolerate to present as an option* in their teaching.

Of course, objective morality, or the Natural Law, is not one among many moral options; it is the very definition of morality. "Subjective morality" is an oxymoron; it is no morality at all; it is a mere game. If I (or we) make rules, I (or we) can change them. If I tie myself up, I am not really bound. And a nonbinding morality is not morality, only "some good ideas". It has no *laws*, nothing with teeth in it; only "values": soft, squooshy things that feel like teddy bears.

C. S. Lewis wrote that moral subjectivism "will certainly end our species and damn our souls". Please remember that Englishmen are not given to exaggeration. He called this "The Abolition of Man". It is fatal. It is like not paying attention to the doctor's diagnosis of your cancer, or like saying to him: "Thank you for sharing your feelings. What makes you think you have a right to impose them on me?" It is like turning off the lights in the operating room and playing fantasy hospital in your head. And this is precisely the orthodoxy of modern Western civilization's three major mind-molding establishments: education, from day-care centers to graduate schools; entertainment, that is, informal education; and journalism.

2. The second principle is that, for the vast majority of all people in all times, places, and cultures, morality, in turn, depends on religion. Only an elite few, like Plato and Aristotle, will ever believe in an absolute morality without an absolute religion. It is theoretically possible to know the effect—the moral law—without knowing the cause—God. But history shows few if any good examples of religionless morality. Our current attempt at a purely rational, secular morality is a leftover hangnail from the Enlightenment (which is the Orwellian name for the Endarkenment). The vast majority of people agree with Dostoyevsky: "If there is no God, everything is permissible." No one has ever given an adequate answer to the simple question: "Why not?" *Why not* do any evil I passionately and sincerely and "authentically" want to do, if there is no superhuman lawmaker and no superhuman law? Only because I might get caught, because "crime doesn't pay"? But crime often *does* pay: well over half of all crimes are never punished. And if the only deterrent is cops, not conscience, what of the conscience of the cops? Who will guard the guards? And how many guards must we have to police a society of immoralists? A state full of moral subjectivists must become a police state. Cops and conscience are the only two effective deterrents to crime. And God is the only guarantor of the authority of conscience. Secular, sociological, "reasonable" answers to the fatal "Why not?" question—like "appropriate behavior" or "utility to the community" or "consensus"—will not deter

us from strongly desired evil. For *why* ought I to care about behaving "appropriately" or about utility to the community or about consensus? If all values are in question, then those halfhearted and apologetic ones certainly won't stand in my way any more than others.

We are beginning, more and more, to ask this fatal question: *Why not?* It is parallel in the moral order to Nietzsche's fatal question about truth: *Why truth? Why not rather untruth?* Suppose I don't like the truth? Why not tell lies and even believe them? Deconstructionists are already daring to say things like that: that "Truth" is only a hypocritical mask on the face of Power.

There is no answer to this attitude unless truth is absolute. The death of God, Nietzsche saw with blinding, prophetic accuracy, was also the death of objective truth. For truth is simply "God without a face". "How can there be eternal truth if there is no eternal mind to think it?" asks Sartre, that pale, professorial copy of Nietzsche.

What happens when society becomes secularized? What happens when God dies? When God dies, His image dies too. The abolition of God entails the abolition of man, the abolition of the specifically human faculty of conscience, God's prophet in the soul. The authority of conscience, like that of any prophet, depends on the authority of God. Why should we revere the King's messenger when we have killed the King?

When a man leaves a room, his image disappears from the mirror in that room. We are living in that split second between the disappearance of God and the disappearance of His image in the human mirror. The image is the life of our souls, our consciences. That is what our present "culture war" is about. It is not merely about getting our rights in the naked public square; it is about the salvation of the soul. It is very probably about the continued biological survival of our species and our civilization on this planet in the next millennium, for the death within will necessarily spill out into a visible death without, like oozing pus. It is certainly about eternal life or eternal death, for without repentance there can be no salvation, and without a real moral law there can be no repentance, and the culture war's Pearl Harbor is the attack on the moral law.

The Obstacles to the Only Possible Solution

So: without religion, no morality, and without morality, no salvation of society or of individuals. *But*: there are two structural obstacles to this solution, this only possible solution. One is the separation between our society and religion, and the other is the separation and split both within the Christian religion and among the religions of the world.

I will mention the first only very briefly, because I have no bright ideas about it at all.

Even though most Americans probably misunderstand what our founding fathers would have meant by the phrase "the separation of Church and state"—a phrase none of them ever used—the basic point seems desirable to most Americans: something desirable for Church as well as for state. Unlike *all* traditional civilizations, we are religiously pluralistic, and our government is religiously neutral.

One question here is whether it is *possible* for a state to be religiously neutral. Another is what this neutrality *means*. Our founding fathers conceived the state's religious "neutrality" as *specific*: no one specific church will be the state church. But our present legal establishment conceives religious neutrality as *generic*: the state will not favor religion as such. Now suppose this is reformed. Suppose we turn back the clock. (As Chesterton tells us, this is a very reasonable and possible thing to do when the clock is keeping very bad time.) Suppose the state supports generic religion again. That is certainly better than the state opposing religion or trying to be neutral (if that is even possible). But it would still be a religiously weaker thing than the older, pre-American system, which was a close linking of the state with one particular religion (Christianity). Generic religion is like generic love: it lacks the passion and power of specificity. It appeals less to ordinary people than to scholars, for whom abstractions are important.

So we have the following trilemma for the state: it supports a specific religion, a solution that is not going to work in a religiously plural society; or it supports generic religion, a solution that is weak; or it supports no religion, a solution that is fatal.

A fourth possible solution is spiritual secession, the creation of a religious subculture. The explosive growth of home schooling seems to be the advance wave of this subculture. This seems to be a wonderful thing for individuals, families, and religious communities. But it leaves the state untouched. If you secede from the mainstream because it is toxic and terminally polluted, the mainstream is doomed. The attempt to reform the state has been abandoned. Perhaps this is all we can do; perhaps it is too late to save the state. But that is not self-evident. Perhaps because I live close to Fenway Park, hope springs eternal (or at lest perennial) in my breast. It is a strange and paradoxical mixture of optimism and pessimism typical of Red Sox fans. One might define it as a pessimism about one's optimism. The definitive example: a Red Sox fan once unfurled a sign on Opening Day: "Wait Till Next Year."

The second problem is apparently even more insoluble. It is that religion speaks with divided and therefore weakened voice. Christianity itself speaks with a tongue forked by the divisions of 1054 and 1517 and by the swords and fires of fratricidal wars. In our half century there has been a remarkable upsurge in the longing for unity. Yet no one can say how to achieve it. The problem is simple and obvious: religions contradict each other. And contradictories cannot both be true. Unity between the true and the false is false unity. Sometimes religions complement each other. But sometimes religions contradict each other. Either God created the world out of nothing and gave it a moral law (as Western religions believe), or He did not (as Eastern religions believe). Either He gave Muhammad the Qur'an, or He did not. Either He chose the Jews, or He did not. Either He became incarnate as Christ, or He did not. Either He founded the Catholic Church, or He did not. And whichever side is wrong about any of these things is very dreadfully wrong about a dreadfully important thing.

When religions contradict each other, the only two logically possible ways to unity seem to be either (a) for one or both sides in each religious dispute to compromise and betray some of its convictions, or (b) for one side to convert the other, to convince the other side of its errors. The first—compromise—is the dream of the liberal and the nightmare of the conservative. The second—conversion—is the dream of the conservative and the nightmare of the liberal. But both seem impossible dreams. True believers aren't going to compromise *or* convert.

So in confronting the disease of the moral decay of modern society with the prescription of religion, we run up against the problem of the plurality of doctors, each with his own medicine: the so-called "problem of comparative religion"—a problem over which tens of thousands of theologians, philosophers, historians, Scripture scholars, and other assorted experts have spilled millions of tons of ink without making a single map to the Promised Land. The only verifiable result of the study of "comparative religions" has been, as Ronald Knox quipped, that it makes you comparatively religious.

The only map the optimists have come up with has been the old picture of "many roads up the same mountain". There are two major problems with this. First, it ignores real contradictions between religions or else denies the law of noncontradiction itself (thus presupposing it, by the way, for in contradicting noncontradiction and preferring contradiction, it assumes a contradiction between noncontradiction and contradiction). Second, it appeals to no one but weak believers in each religion, for the picture of religions as many roads up the mountain assumes that religions are man-made yogas, not God-made revelations; useful, not true; therapy, not prophecy. But all three Western religions claim to be God's definitive road down, not one of man's many nondefinitive roads up.

A Hindu can easily "accept" Christianity as another *bhakti yoga*, but how can a Christian accept Hinduism as another way of salvation? No guru ever claimed that no one could come to the Father except through him. A Catholic accepts the Protestant principle of the infallibility of Scripture, but how can he add *sola* to *scriptura* without denying the claims of the Church? A Protestant can accept a Catholic's faith in Christ, but how can he accept or respect what he considers an egregious and idolatrous error—bowing to bread, worshipping a wafer that the Church insists is God incarnate? And how can a Jew or a Muslim accept the very essence of Christianity, Christ Himself as God, and thus the Trinity, without betraying his own religion? Clearly, these things are not possible. Each must believe that the others are making terrible errors about the things that matter most of all; or else they must cease to believe that and become indifferent, reducing religion to a kind of transcendental pop psychology.

What can we do to solve this problem? If we are honest, the answer is: Nothing. Nothing that we can see.

How God Solves the Insoluble

We turn now from what we can do to what God is doing.

God has a way of changing the very parameters of our problems. Often, within those parameters, there is no solution. For instance, the Pharisees ask Jesus: Should we withhold tax money from Caesar the tyrant or not? If He says Yes, He violates Roman law; if He says No, He offends Jewish law. Should we stone the adulteress or not? If He says Yes, He offends mercy, if He says No, He offends justice. Also in this second case, if He says Yes, He violates Roman law, which did not grant the Jews the right of capital punishment; but if He says No, He violates Mosaic law, which commanded capital punishment for this crime. And if He says nothing, He cops out. Within the terms of the problem, there is no possible answer.

The stunning style of His answers is well known (see Mt 22:15–22; Jn 8:1–11).

What is their common source? That God is not confined to the terms of any human problem; that no cage can contain Christ the Tiger.

Take the man beside the pool of Bethesda (Jn 5). He *needs* the healing that only the angel-troubled water of the pool can give him *because he is crippled*; but he can't get into the pool to *get* the healing *because he is crippled*. Catch-22. There is no possible solution within the logical parameters of the problem. Jesus cuts through those parameters like the sword through the Gordian knot, and He heals the man instantly.

What is impossible for man is possible for God. It is impossible for us to solve the tangled problem of comparative religions. It is also impossible, it seems, to win the war against secularization and moral relativism that has been the main story of Western civilization since the end of the Middle Ages, especially since the Enlightenment, more especially in this, the devil's century (according to Pope Leo XIII's vision), and most especially of all since the sexual revolution of the sixties. And so God, I suggest, is working right now to deal with both problems with the same stroke, which I will call "ecumenical jihad". The age of religious war*s* is ending; the age of religious *war* is beginning: a war of all religions against none. The First World War of Religion is upon us.

Pope John Paul II has said that the third millennium may be the millennium of Christian unity, as the second millennium was the millennium of Christian disunity. A suspiciously providential three-stage structure of Church history thus opens up before our gaze, corresponding to the three stages of all human history according to Scripture: creation, fall, and redemption, or Paradise, Paradise Lost, and Paradise Regained. First, we won the world. Then, we lost it. Then, we must win it again.

The first millennium was the millennium of Christian unity. There was one and only one worldwide visible Church from Pentecost until 1054.

The second millennium was the millennium of Christian disunity: tears in Christ's seamless garment: 1054, 1517, and all the further tears that followed 1517. The Body of Christ seemed to the world to be dying. For when the organs of a body no longer work together, the body dies.

But this is Christ's Body, and therefore it rises from its graves. Perhaps, in the wonderful plotting of divine providence, the third millennium will be the millennium of the resurrection of unity, or reunification.

In this scenario, the return to a pagan, non-Christian world outside the Church will elicit the divine response of a return to a unified Church to confront this world. The plethora of forces from the second millennium seem to be coalescing into these two as we enter the third millennium— rather like the Marxist theory of history, in which the decisive revolution can happen only when the many classes of pre-Capitalist society coalesce into only two classes under Capitalism. Marx's Proletariat and Bourgeoisie correspond to Augustine's City of God and City of the World.

We have no crystal ball. But we have clues—many clues, both a priori clues and a posteriori clues. A priori, does not every human story pass through these three stages—stages of some kind of creation, fall, and redemption? The structure of every story is that a situation is first set up, then upset, then reset (whether happily or unhappily). And a posteriori, we seem to see the shift from stage two to stage three beginning to take shape under our eyes, not only in a newly unified anti-Church world, but also in a newly unified anti-world Church.

The battle lines are obviously changing. No longer are Protestants and Catholics anathematizing each other. Relations with Jews and even Muslims are beginning to show signs of understanding and respect never before seen in history. Our hearts, if not our heads, are in fact being brought closer together, and it seems that our divine Commander's strategy is to bring this change about by confronting us with the increasingly clear and present danger of the common enemy, the new tower of Babel. Nothing unites like a common enemy and a common emergency. A blizzard makes neighbors into friends. War can make even enemies into friends. Some of the Irish volunteered to risk their lives in the trenches of two World Wars side by side with their hated English overlords and enemies because, compared with the global threat of German barbarism, their local British civil war seemed an unaffordable luxury. Feuding brothers stop feuding when a maniac invades their house. God seems to

have let the maniac Satan loose, or rather slackened His hold
on Satan's leash, as He did in the case of Job, for a very
definite purpose. Ever since Judas betrayed Christ and thus
made our salvation possible, God has been using Satan to
undo Satan. He has now allowed Satan to let loose upon the
world a worldwide spiritual war, which by attacking not one
religion but all religions is now uniting God-loving Catholics, Orthodox, Anglicans, and Protestants (and even Jews
and Muslims) more powerfully than anything else in history
has ever done. The delicious irony of it all is that the very
brilliance of Satan's strategy is destined to defeat Satan now
as it did before with Judas. Satan's strategy was to divide and
conquer. And because he has divided, he is conquering.
And because he is conquering, we are uniting to defeat him.
So because he has divided us, he is uniting us.

Of course, even if this invisible scenario for the cosmic
jihad is accurate, it does not solve a single one of the classic
theoretical and theological problems of comparative religion.
It does not make it possible for a Catholic to accept *sola
scriptura* or for a Protestant to accept papal infallibility. What it
does is make them love each other and fight side by side to
the death for the love of the same Christ. Is that a lesser
achievement or a greater one?

What theological and ecclesiastical solutions will emerge
from this new situation and this new alliance? No one can
tell, because the alliance is still in the early stages of formation. That formation is in a clearer and more advanced stage
in front of abortuaries and in inner-city drug centers than it is
in the churches or seminaries or universities. Practice is leading theory.

Of course, ecumenism is not homogeneous. We must
clearly distinguish at least five specifically different kinds or
levels of ecumenism. The distinction must be made both in
theory, or belief, and in practice, or cooperation in a com-

mon jihad against our common foe "who seeks to work us woe".

First, there is Christian ecumenism. This is the only etymologically and theologically proper sense of the word. Cooperation among Christian churches is based most fundamentally on the fact that the same single, indivisible Christ is the energizing center of all Christians; that in God's eyes, and therefore in true reality, the Body of Christ is still one because it is eternally one, though its visible appearance is now split. Christ is not divided, only His seamless garment is. The Mystical Body of Christ cannot be divided. His Bride cannot be plural, for He is not a polygamist. When He comes again (and may it be soon!), He will not marry a harem.

Cooperation among Christians is based also on the fact that we are commanded to "be of one mind . . . the mind of Christ". It is not only our will but His "that they may be one." As John Paul has said in his encyclical on ecumenism (*Ut unum sint*), ecumenism is not an option; it is an order. It comes, not from theologians, but from *Theos*.

Second, there is Jewish-Christian ecumenism. Mutual love and cooperation can happen here, but unification can take place only through Christians apostatizing or Jews converting. It is not certain that unity between Rome and Constantinople or Geneva or Canterbury can take place only by apostasy or conversion. Christian ecumenism is between squabbling siblings; Jewish–Christian ecumenism is between estranged parent and child. Yet the Jews remain our fathers in the faith, the only "other" religion that is in no way "other" to us, the only one we fully accept as divinely revealed and infallible.

Third, there is Christian-Muslim ecumenism. This is even more difficult, not only because historically Muslims have resisted conversion more than any other people, but because while Jewish converts to Christ become completed Jews,

Muslim converts do not become completed Muslims. Nothing in the Jewish Scriptures contradicts Christianity, but some things in the Qur'an do. Yet even here, an "ecumenical jihad" is possible and is called for, for the simple and strong reason that Muslims and Christians preach and practice the same First Commandment: *islam*, total surrender, submission of the human will to the divine will. We fight side by side not only because we face a common enemy but above all because we serve and worship the same divine Commander.

Many Christians, both Protestant and Catholic, do not believe what the Church says about Islam (for example, in Vatican II and in the new *Catechism*): that Allah is not another God, that we worship the same God. Once, after debating the existence of God with an atheist and having spent a good deal of time explicating and defending the divine attributes, I was approached by a Muslim from the audience, who said to me, "It does my heart good to hear such good Islamic orthodoxy. You are a Muslim, aren't you?" He could not believe I was a Christian, because, he said, "You truly know Allah." Apparently he had thought (contrary to the Qur'an) that Christians worshipped a different God. These misunderstandings had better be cleared up, or great battlefield confusion between friend and foe will result.

Fourth, there is ecumenical unity with other religions that do not know the God of Abraham: Hinduism and Buddhism, for instance. Many of the battlefields of the great war reach this far. For instance, Hindus and Buddhists joined Catholic, Protestant, Jewish, and Muslim clergy in protesting "designer genes"—creating bits of humanity in laboratories for experimenting on, for "harvesting" organs, or for manipulating and redesigning human nature itself. There is a fundamental fissure, a Grand Canyon, between secularists who acknowledge no law above human desire and *all* the religions of the world.

Finally, even atheists and agnostics, if they are of good will and intellectual honesty and still believe in objective truth and objective morality, are on our side in the war against the powers of darkness. Perhaps they can be called "anonymous Christians", as Karl Rahner suggested (following Saint Justin Martyr); or perhaps this is a theological confusion. But in any case they cannot be called warriors for the Antichrist. If they seek the truth, they will find it, eventually. Of that we are assured by Christ Himself. They may not yet be married to God, but they are not deliberate divorcées either. Dr. Bernard Nathanson is not in the same army as Madeline Murray O'Hare.

I have no idea what new theological understanding might emerge from this new practical moral alliance; but I think that such an understanding will happen. For love causes knowledge. Orthopraxy leads to orthodoxy, as well as vice versa. Unity in action opens new eyes to understanding unity in thought. This is the principle taught by Dostoyevsky in *The Brothers Karamazov* when he has his wise old *starets*, Father Zossima, hear the confession of Madame Hohlokov, "a lady of little faith", who has lost her faith through an "Enlightenment" education, thinks everything can be explained by science and matter, and is terrified that when she dies there will be "only the burdocks on my grave". She asks how she can get her faith back. And Father Zossima tells her, in effect, that orthopraxy will lead to orthodoxy. Just as faith can lead to good works—to charity—so charity can lead to faith. "Love your neighbor indefatigably, and you will come to see the immortality of his soul. This has been tried. This is certain." But (Zossima warns) it has to be real and costly love; charity, not simply spontaneous human feeling or "compassion". "I am sorry I can tell you nothing more comforting. For love in action is a harsh and dreadful thing compared with love in dreams."

Apparently the woman fails the test, for she is one of those who has grand schemes for the salvation of "humanity" but can't stand her next-door neighbor, especially when he gets too close. We, however, need not fail the test. If we will work and fight and love in action side by side with our Protestant and Catholic and Orthodox and Jewish and Muslim neighbors, we will come to perceive something we did not understand before. What will it be? We do not yet know. We will be able to perceive it only by working the works of love and war, not by speculating.

Some Specific Clues:
Pearls on the Thread of God's Strategy

Here are some more specific pieces of evidence for my basic contention that divine providence is introducing us into this new age of "ecumenical jihad".

Any *one* of the following fifteen events should be cause for rejoicing and for thinking that there is a radical change of battle lines. All of them together, when seen together and connected under this theme, make an overwhelming case— *fifteen* fingerprints of the same divine finger.

1. Let's begin with the remarkable fact that in the period 1992–95, perhaps half the people in America have finally awakened to the simple, crucial realization that we are at war. Before the presidential election of 1992, the only ones who thought we were in a spiritual war, or even a culture war, were a small minority whom the media effectively dismissed as extremists. But today, awareness of the "culture war" is common. The fog—Satan's most powerful weapon—is lifting. Light is dawning. The truth-tumor is rapidly metastasizing.

2. More specifically and locally, we have only to look at the 1994 elections: not a single pro-life candidate lost to a pro-

abortion candidate in the Senate or the House or in a guber-
natorial election. The so-called "social issues", scorned by
the experts, clearly rank first in the minds of the people. The
next few years will test whether we have a government of the
experts, by the experts, and for the experts or a government
of the people, by the people, and for the people.

3. What the media call (with holy terror) "the rise of the
Religious Right" is a formidable phenomenon, one no one
expected twenty years ago. And it's not going away.

4. Within the Roman Catholic Church we have a Pope
who knows where the battles are and who fights like a great,
gentle bear—a new Gregory the Great. He has surely done
more than anyone in our century to save the world from
Communism and from nuclear war. He fights with a formidable array of weapons: holiness, will power, intelligence,
preaching, philosophizing, writing, politicking, and prophetic foresight. He is a spiritual Pericles, a winner of un-
winnable battles.

5. The United Nations 1994 Cairo conference on population control, for instance. Who could have predicted it? Who
did? The plans of the powerful secular establishment, sup-
ported by the U.S., the U.N., vastly superior funding, and a
totalitarian programmatic organization, were defeated by—a
coalition of the Vatican and Islamic countries! Has such a
coalition ever taken place before? What could have occa-
sioned it? Only awareness of a common supernatural war
against a common supernatural enemy who hates the sanctity
of life and who wants to destroy unborn babies, femininity,
masculinity, families, and chastity. I would call Cairo (and its
echoes at Beijing a year later) a greater victory *with* Islam than
the Battle of Lepanto was *against* it.

6. Within the Catholic Church, Satan's new strategy has
been to fill the ranks of middle management—where pastoral
decisions especially in education are made—with spies. (We

used to call them "heretics", but we no longer dare to use that word because we are rightly embarrassed at our mistake in burning them. However, there is no need to fear the reinstitution of the crude device of burning at the stake, since modern technology has given us cryogenics, so we can now freeze them instead and thaw them out when the Parousia arrives.) A whole generation of Catholic catechumens has been suddenly and catastrophically lost. Most have never even been taught how to get to Heaven, much less the meaning of the Trinity or the Incarnation. But the satanic strategy is now beginning to backfire, for the Church is an organism, and the organism is producing antibodies. Nearly all the interesting new Catholic writers are orthodox; nearly all the orthodox seminaries are bursting full while the liberal ones are drearily empty; dozens of new Catholic magazines are appearing, all robustly orthodox; and truly orthodox Catholic colleges are springing up, schools that are clearly the wave of the future: Steubenville, Saint Thomas Aquinas, Saint Thomas More, Christendom—soon even an ecumenical Evangelical and Catholic Great Books School, C. S. Lewis College.

7. Lewis himself is a phenomenon. Without the slightest compromise or watering-down of the claims of any church or denomination, he showed to millions of readers that "mere Christianity" is a real and solid center, not a lowest-common-denominator abstraction, and that it is far more attractive and defensible and interesting than anything else in the world. His appeal increases every year.

It is hard for us to realize how far we have come in being able to see that clearly, hard for us to realize that as recently as forty years ago most Catholics *and* most Protestants would have been surprised, confused, or even scandalized to hear what all now see as obvious: that Cardinal O'Connor is closer to Jerry Falwell than to Hans Küng and that an orthodox Southern Baptist has more in common with the Pope than with a Modernist Baptist. For whether Christ is the Savior is more important than whether the Pope is His vicar; and whether there is one Savior or many is more important than whether there are two sacraments or seven. In dividing each church, the Modernists have begun to unite all churches against Modernism.

8. From the beginning of his pontificate, John Paul looked East: both to his enemy, Communism, and to his friend, Orthodoxy. When he was first elected, he said he had three great tasks: defeating Communism and the threat of nuclear war, effecting reunion with Orthodoxy, and reforming the Church in America. The first was relatively easy, the third may prove impossible. But the second, I think, is closest to his heart. How can the Church breathe with only one of her two lungs? he has often asked. No previous Pope has ever been as adamant about that.

9. I was amazed to find out (at a Luther-Aquinas conference) that most Lutherans seriously hope for eventual reunion with Rome. The single major obstacle, the thing that could not be compromised and that justified Luther in his own mind for the terrible act of tearing apart the visible fabric of Christ's Body, was of course the doctrine of justification by faith, close to the very heart of the gospel. Well, the joint statement by the Vatican and the German Lutheran bishops about ten years ago announced, in effect, that we are not really divided there; that that problem is solved; that both churches agree in substance, though using different terminology. It took us four and a half centuries and many bloody wars to see it, but there it is.

When Tom Howard became a Catholic, Gordon College fired him because it required all faculty members to believe and sign a statement of faith that included the tenet of justification by faith. I had been teaching there part time, too, and the College told Tom and me that although we had both signed their statement, we could not teach there inasmuch as we could not really believe it because we were Catholics. When we both protested that we did indeed believe this tenet (how could we not—it's in our data, Scripture!), the administrators simply could not understand this. So they gave us a friendly little lecture on what Catholics believed.

Each year, there are fewer and fewer Protestants and Catholics who are misled by that old misunderstanding. It is becoming clear to both sides that we are saved only by Christ, by grace; that faith is our acceptance of that grace, so we are saved by faith; and that good works, the works of love, necessarily follow from that faith if it is real and saving faith, so we cannot be saved by a faith without good works. Both sides agree with this, because both sides accept the scriptural data, and the solution is right there in the data. Unity always comes about by a return to the sources, to the data.

Unfortunately, there are still many who don't even know the data, the gospel. Most of my Catholic students at Boston College have never heard it. When I ask them what they would say to God if they died tonight and God asked them why He should take them into Heaven, nine out of ten do not even mention Jesus Christ. Most of them say they have been good, or kind, or sincere, or did their best. So I seriously doubt God will undo the Reformation until He sees to it that Luther's reminder of Paul's gospel has been heard throughout the Church.

10. The "Evangelicals and Catholics Together" statement (May, 1994), while solving no theological problems, was also a major new step, a great air-cleanser and fog-dispeller and proper-perspective-restorer.

11. The Vatican also has taken Reformed tradition more seriously than ever before, especially in dialoguing with it continually in the German bishops' catechism that came out in 1985.

12. Protestant Fundamentalists who formerly fulminated fire from the mouth at the Church as the Whore of Babylon have been seen marching and praying side by side with Catholics before abortion clinics and going with them to jail. Sharing a prison cell unites you much more powerfully than sharing a conference table.

13. Representatives from all the major religions of the world met and prayed together for a peace at Assisi (October 27, 1986). A small step, perhaps, but *such a thing had never happened before in the history of the world.*

14. Catholic-Jewish relations have become notably closer, especially after Vatican II's *Nostra aetate* officially told Catholics it was wrong to single out the Jews to blame for the crucifixion and after the Vatican's recognition of the State of Israel. This relationship is crucial, since it is between the only two visible religious entities we know will last till the end of time: a visible Israel and the visible Church. Israel is a central channel or conduit of divine providence in world history.

15. And Islam, our ancient foe, is beginning to become our friend. If we did not balk at having Stalin's followers as our allies against Hitler, we surely should not balk at having Muhammad's followers as our allies against Satan. The new alliance emerged most notably at Cairo, but there were little hints before that. For instance, when the British Broadcasting Corporation ran a blasphemous skit about Christ, the Muslims demanded and got an apology, whereas Christians remained silent. A telling example from my own experience: it took a Muslim student in my class at Boston College to berate the Catholics for taking down their crucifixes. "We don't have images of that man, as you do," he said, "but if we did, we would never take them down, even if someone tried to force us to. We revere that man, and we would die for his honor. But you are so ashamed of him that you take him down from your walls. You are more afraid of what his

enemies might think if you kept your crucifixes up than of what *he* might think if you took them down. So I think we are better Christians than you are."

How dare we be worse Christians than Muslims are!

Why is Islam expanding so spectacularly? Sociologists and psychologists and historians and economists and demographers and politicians are quick to explain this growth with "expert" worldly wisdom from each of their specialties; but to any Christian familiar with the Bible, the answer is obvious: because God keeps His promises and blesses those who obey His laws and fear Him and punishes those who do not. Much too simple for scholars to see. Compare the amounts of abortion, adultery, fornication, and sodomy among Muslims and among Christians. Then compare the amounts of prayer.

Prescription

If my analysis is true, what follows? What should we do, and what will it accomplish? What is my prescription, and what is my prognosis?

My prescription is a more conscious and deliberate alliance against our common enemy, an alliance that will channel our energies away from our civil wars against each other and into this common world war. But is this prescription legitimate? Does it not ignore real and important "civil war" issues?

The alliance is tactical, not theoretical. It is not a religious syncretism or indifference. It is an *alliance*. Allies do not give up their sovereignty or their individuality. They simply put their disputes on hold for tactical, practical reasons. Such tactical moves are matters of prudential wisdom. I think it is very likely that the time will soon come—perhaps it is already here—when the emergency is so great that prudence dictates a moratorium on our polemics against each other and our attempts to convert each other—not because these attempts are not honest and honorable activities, but because the heat of battle may soon require us to spend all our energies against our common enemy, for the sake of the salvation of millions of souls and of global human society.

To call for such a halt to criticisms of each other is *not* to call for indifferentism. Nor is it a hidden plan to create a single world religion. Nor is it a way to solve any of our real and important theological and ecclesial problems. It is none of these things, not because it is something weaker and thus less threatening, but because it is even more powerful and important. It is a matter of life or death, eternal life or eternal death, Heaven or Hell for millions of souls, man's conquest of Satan or Satan's conquest of man.

Our common Commander has issued a common promise: obedience brings victory. The essential prescription for victory is the simplest possible, both in religion and in war: obey your commanding officer. Bow the whole heart and head and knee to God. Without the slightest doubt or compromise of your particular faith—Protestant, Orthodox, Catholic, Jewish—practice *islam*: total and absolute submission and surrender to God's will. Offer yourself for whatever role He will have you play in His battle plan—even if it turns out to be none. Make out a blank check to God. Each of these faiths at its very center commands us to do just that. So all I am proposing we do is a more resolute and clear-minded doing of what we already admit we should above all do.

We all know the positive answer to "What should we do?" But we may need to be reminded of something we should *not* do. We should not make ecumenism our aim, our goal. No abstract ideal is our aim. Christianity is not an idealism, it is a realism. Truth is not an abstraction; truth is a Person: truth is Jesus Christ. We do not serve a future ideal but a present Lord. The Word of God is not a "message"; it is a Person. Let us not sell our birthright for a pot of message.

As Christianity is not man's search for God but God's search for man, so Christian ecumenism must be not man's search for unity but God's work. As the "Evangelicals and Catholics Together" statement put it, "we have not chosen one another; we have been chosen."

Prognosis

What will happen if we take this prescription? What prognosis follows?

I am sure of only one thing: that if we let God have His way, He will surprise us. He will do something we will not have predicted, something wonderful, something in fact Godlike, something eye has not seen, something ear has not heard, something that has not entered into the heart of man, something that would make the hairs on our neck stand up and our ears tremble.

His style is always to outguess us, to do something more wonderful than we could ever have imagined. Always, He can say: "Behold, I do a new thing!"

If *we* were pure spirits, would we ever have come up with the idea of creating matter?

And how did Omnipotence ever invent the idea of creating beings with free will who could defy Him?

Above all, who ever could have predicted the Incarnation, the most incredible, astonishing, impossible event in all time, what Kierkegaard calls "the absolute paradox"? How could anyone ever have thought that the God whose unchangeable essence is to be eternal and not to have a cause or a beginning in time or a body should have a cause and a beginning in time and a body through a creature, the Virgin Mary? How could any theist ever have thought of calling a woman "the Mother of God"?

And how could the deathless God die? How could *hagios athanatos* give up the ghost?

And His saints, who reproduce the life of Christ—they are similarly unpredictable. And His Church—He will heal her as unpredictably as He founded her. We do not know how. Whatever He will do, it will be far better and wiser and more wonderful than the best any of us could imagine.

Will Christ solve the problem of comparative religions? Will He give us the unity we long for? Yes, in His time. Perhaps this is the beginning of that time, or perhaps this is not yet that time, or perhaps that time will not come until Heaven. But in time, the practice of total submission to God's will will necessarily solve the problem of comparative religions, will necessarily create among us the unity we know we lack and need, whatever form that unity might take. Why "necessarily"? It's a simple syllogism:

> The practice of submission to God's will means letting God's will be done.
> God has told us (for example, in John 17) that His will for us is unity.
> Therefore submission to His will *will* lead to unity.

The way to make one harmonious music is for all the players in the orchestra to obey the conductor's baton.

If and when we do, what music will He make? Let Him do it, and you will see.

Chapter Two

A Christian Defense of Jihad

Many a Christian reader of this book thus far is likely to criticize me for sounding more like a Muslim than a Christian. My response is: By "Christian", do you mean "harmless wimp"? Granted that most Muslims fail to understand the Christian paradox that *suffering love* is the most powerful of all weapons in spiritual warfare, is it not equally true, alas, that most Christians in America today also fail to understand the Christian paradox that suffering love *is the most powerful of all weapons in spiritual warfare*? Are Muslims the only ones left who smell the smoke of battle or the only ones who are still eager to enlist in God's army?

Mainline American Christians are likely to object that my position is "too polemical". Let's consider some specific forms of that objection.

Objection 1: If you emphasize spiritual war, it inevitably turns into literal, physical war. Look at the Muslims with their "jihads".

Reply: As a matter of fact, only a small minority of Muslims worldwide identify jihad with physical violence, and our media gleefully swoop down on the opportunity to tar them all with this Fundamentalist brush—the same glee with which they swoop down on Jim and Tammy Faye Bakker and priestly pedophiles.

But the substantive answer to the objection is simple: *Abusus non tollit usum*. The abuse does not take away the (proper) use. There is nothing distinctive here about the doctrine of spiritual warfare: *every* Christian doctrine is dangerous and destructive when abused. That's why we need the Church: to tame this heart of wild tigers (to use Chesterton's image).

Two opposite errors are always possible. For "there is one angle at which to stand upright, but many angles at which to fall." (That's another insight from Chesterton. He is like potato chips: you can't eat just one.) Our typically modern error is insensitivity to the hard virtues: courage, self-discipline, self-denial, chastity, passionate honesty. The typical error of our ancestors was insensitivity to the soft virtues: compassion, sensitivity to the weak and handicapped, kindness. They would be as shocked at our self-indulgence as we are at their cruelty. Let us avoid *both* errors instead of falling into the devil's trap of arguing which one is worse, thus half-justifying the other.

Objection 2: Talk about war fills you with hate. Christians are supposed to be filled with love, not with hateful talk about war and enemies.

Reply: If Christianity means what Christ taught, then Christians are supposed to love their enemies. How can you love your enemies if you have no enemies?

The key principle, which avoids both the "soft" and "hard" errors, is to "love the sinner but hate the sin." That principle used to be well known. Many today have never heard it. Many reject it. Many sinners explicitly argue that if you hate their sin, you hate them.

For some reason, I have never heard this argument about

anything except sexual sin, usually sodomy. I do not understand why it is only certain apologists for *this* sin who so identify their whole selves with their "lifestyle" that they refuse even to distinguish their very selves from their sins. It is a terrifying sort of identification, of course, no matter what the sin, for that is almost exactly the definition of Hell.

Of course the more you love the sinner the more you hate and make war on the sin, just as the more you love the person, the more you hate and kill the cancer cells that are killing the person. Compassion for cancer cells does not come from compassion for persons; it comes precisely from *lack* of compassion for persons.

Objection 3: This is rhetoric rather than responsible, objective, scholarly analysis. Furthermore, it is polemical rhetoric and therefore dangerous.

Reply: It *is* rhetoric rather than scholarly analysis; an alarm bell rather than a sonata; an imitation of Demosthenes rather than of Cicero. (When Cicero addressed the Senate, everyone said, "How beautifully he speaks!" but remained seated. When Demosthenes addressed his troops, they all stood and said, "Let us march!") When we are at war and in danger of dying, we need marchers, and speechmakers to motivate marchers.

Objection 4: Spiritual warfare is not central or essential to Christianity. Charity is.

Reply: In a sin-filled world, charity *is* an act of spiritual warfare. When divine love incarnates itself East of Eden, it forms a Cross. At the center of Christianity is the Cross. The Cross is indeed a symbol of charity—stunning, shattering charity. It is also clearly a symbol of spiritual warfare. It is shaped like a sword held at the hilt by the hand of Heaven and stuck into the earth, not to draw blood but to give it.

Objection 5: But Christ came to bring peace. We should work for peace.

Reply: He also said He came to bring a sword. He did not come to bring us the peace that the world gives. He explicitly said that. He clearly distinguished His peace from the world's peace, just as He clearly distinguished His love from the world's love, saying that all men would know and recognize and distinguish His disciples by the new kind of love they had for each other. The peace the world gives is saying Yes to the world, the flesh, and the devil. The peace Christ gives is saying Yes to poverty, chastity, and obedience and therefore No to the world, the flesh, and the devil. The peace Christ brought, the peace the world cannot give, is a peace with neighbor, with self, and with God. This peace means making war on greed and lust and pride, which are the enemies of peace with neighbor, self, and God. The two forms of peace are exact opposites. They are at war with each other. All saints knew and lived this truth. If we don't, that's why we are not saints.

Let me quote a letter to a Catholic journal from an ordinary Catholic woman: "We're always being told to pray for peace. I wonder: Aren't we allowed to pray for *victory* any more? We're supposed to be 'the Church Militant', fighting against the powers of darkness. Since there's no shortage of darkness, I think we should be allowed to pray for victory."

Yes, we're supposed to be the Church Militant. And we sound more like the Church Mumbling.

Objection 6: The only Christlike form of spiritual warfare is service, not aggression. God emptied Himself and became a slave, not a warrior.

Reply: That is exactly right. But a slave first of all to the Father, not to the *Zeitgeist*. A slave obeys his master. Our divine Master commands us to do what Christ did: to aggress on sin, though not on sinners. And first of all our own sins. If we are not racists but are fornicators, it does us no good to make war on racism (or vice versa). It is easy to be warlike against unfashionable evils, especially when they are far away. It is less easy to be warlike against fashionable evils or ones close to home.

Christ the slave *is* Christ the warrior. The prototypical Christian act is martyrdom, and martyrs are warriors as well as slaves. Joan Andrews is a warrior. If one hundred bishops went to jail with Joan Andrews, abortion would be conquered. Yes, our weapon is not power but suffering love, but suffering love is *our weapon*. And it is the most powerful weapon in the world. It saved the world from Hell two thousand years ago. It can certainly save it from the American Civil Liberties Union today.

Objection 7: Doesn't this talk of war instead of peace contradict Vatican II? Aren't you proposing a return to a Trent-like model of polemics?

Reply: No, just the opposite. I am suggesting that the Holy Spirit in the Church is orchestrating an even more radical revision of Tridentine strategy than we think. Let me try to explain this suggestion.

Most of us thought at the time that Vatican II was a kind of loosening. I think we can now see that it was also a kind of tightening, a tightening of our belts for battle, a girding of loins. We thought it made the faith less polemical than

Trent because it did not anathematize heretics. But in fact it was preparing us for a greater polemic than Trent's: not against Protestants, our separated brethren, but against the City of the World; not the civil war, but the world war. Why did divine providence lead John XXIII to convene Vatican II, and Vatican II to write *Lumen gentium*, and *Lumen gentium* to call for a new openness to non-Catholic religions? I think at least partly for this strategical, global, polemical reason. God, who knew the future, was preparing for battle. He saw that the enemy was so formidable and so global that this was the providential time to turn our energy away from our local, in-house battles and gather our allies against the devil's axis.

Objection 8: Aren't you overdoing it a bit, exaggerating for the sake of drama?

Reply: How could anyone "overdo" the survival of the human race? That's what is at stake. Do we really expect God to allow a civilization that enshrines Moloch-worship by the deliberate murder of millions of God's beloved babies in the womb to go on indefinitely? God is patient, but "God is not mocked." As my friend in New Orleans puts it, "Don't mess with the Main Man. Don't diss the Deity." The cup of divine wrath must be drunk somehow, somewhere, sometime. Or, to put the same point in other, less scriptural, and less offensive terms, the necessary laws of human nature that all civilizations before ours knew—Natural Law, Tao, Rta, Dike, Karma, "the will of Heaven"—make it impossible to get away with murder. Our most complete channel of knowledge of what God feels and thinks, sweet Jesus, had some pretty terrifying words about those who led His little children astray—something about millstones. I think it is not a very safe bet that He has changed since then and become more tolerant toward those who collaborate in *murdering* His little children.

Objection 9: By your polemics you are being divisive and exclusionary rather than unifying

Reply: It is this polemic, this jihad, that *is* unifying. God is raising an army, forging a new alliance of all who hate evil. This new alliance may prove to be more unifying than anything else in the history of religions. Perhaps all the world's religions will eventually be united in this cause; but so far, in the West, we can see this army being made up of five religious groups, all of which are consistently vilified and libeled in the establishment media because they are the only five identifiable groups in our society who have not bought into the sexual revolution and its offspring, abortion: orthodox Catholics, Evangelical and Fundamentalist Protestants, Muslims, religious Jews, and Eastern Orthodox (the latter not quite as socially prominent and well known, and thus not quite as threatening to the media, but just as adamant and "unprogressive"). Perhaps these five kings of orthodoxy are the five good kings of the Battle of Armageddon?

The longing for religious unity has echoed down four decades of dreamy optimism. Perhaps it will be forged only in the heat of hellish battle. What could not be accomplished irenically may be accomplished polemically.

Objection 10: You are demonizing your opponents.

Reply: You cannot demonize a demon, any more than you can personalize a person. Our enemies *are* demons. We have been clearly told that in Scripture. The theme of supernatural spiritual warfare runs from Genesis through Revelation. It is on every page.

Flesh and blood are not our enemies but our patients. We are God's nurses. Our enemies are the invisible viruses killing our flesh-and-blood patients.

Objection 11: You are being aggressive. Just wars are defensive, not aggressive.

Reply: Against flesh and blood, yes. Against evil, no. We must be more, not less, aggressive against evil.

And defense can be as passionate as aggression: observe any mother in the animal kingdom.

Objection 12: Your model sounds more like something from Archie Bunker than like something from Christ.

Reply: Models are important. The fear of being passionate and polemical often stems from the fear of becoming like those abusive fathers who play god and push around their wives and children like poker chips or swat them like insect pests. But it is true polemics to fight against that very thing. Just war is in the service of peace.

Jesus, our model, said: "I am the good shepherd." The Good Shepherd fights the wolves because He loves the sheep. Not to fight the wolves is not to love the sheep.

Objection 13: You major in minors. You emphasize courage, the military virtue, more than charity.

Reply: I emphasize courage because we have forgotten we need it. We have not forgotten we need charity. We hear that every other sermon, and rightly so. But when do we hear of the need for courage? If there is one virtue conspicuous by its absence from modern life in that protected bubble, the self-indulgent consumerist paradise that is America, it must be courage.

This was what the prophet Alexander Solzhenitsyn said when he came to Harvard in 1978—that the West had lost its courage. And if you doubt the decadence of Western civilization, I ask you to read the whining and sniveling reactions published by the *New York Times* the day after his speech.

One wins even physical wars with spiritual weapons, with courage more than with arms. That eminently practical wisdom is in our Scriptures too, remember—all that the Psalms say about how useless physical weapons like horses and chariots are without spiritual weapons like faith and courage and resolution. It works! Our faith and courage and resolution defeated Hitler and the vilest military machine in history, and our lack of national resolution then led to our defeat by Ho Chi Minh.

Courage is not only the specifically military virtue. It is also a virtue you need for any other virtue, for all virtues take effort and sacrifice. Especially charity. Charity without courage dies, like faith without works.

Objection 14: We haven't heard much from you about compassion.

Reply: Most people are confused about compassion, as they are about love. They confuse both love and compassion with feelings. But feelings are not virtues. Even feelings of sympathy and compassion, though good, are not virtues. The compassion that is a virtue is the compassion God has and commands us to have. Feelings can't be commanded. Choices and deeds can.

Feelings are often substitutes for virtue. Walker Percy wrote the astonishing comment that "compassion led to the [Nazi] death camps." He meant, I think, that the substitution of the feeling of compassion and the "compassionate" quality-of-life ethic for the hard, courageous sanctity-of-life ethic among German intellectuals had already paved the way for Hitler. Compassion for what was called "life unworthy of life" had led to euthanasia, and that was the quality-of-life camel's nose under the tent. After the nose followed the more rearward, smelly part of the camel. It's a one-piece camel. First it was the hopelessly ill who were eliminated, then the suffering, then the severely retarded, then the "inferior" races and the politically incorrect.

"Compassion" for mothers is the reason most often given for butchering babies before birth. Hard reason asks: Why not after? Have we no compassion for mothers of unwanted babies outside the womb, who are even more bothersome to their parents? No reason but only sentiment holds back the inevitable extension of abortion to infanticide. And where is the dividing line between unwanted infant and unwanted child, or unwanted teenager? Surely teenagers make parents suffer as much as babies do. So do old folks. Why not be compassionate to those who are suffering because of unwanted teenagers or unwanted parents? Might the Menendez brothers' case be the harbinger of the future? The thought of slaughtering born people is still shocking to most people now. But the thought of slaughtering unborn babies was equally shocking to most people only a short time ago. How long will it take for the rest of the camel to enter the tent? Eventually, the "compassionate" demand for a world without suffering will necessitate the most ruthless extermination of anyone or anything that causes or reminds us of suffering.

That's the idea-enemy we're fighting.

Chapter Three

A Defense of Fanaticism

To explain why, in calling for a jihad, I am not a "fanatic" requires a whole chapter to itself.

"Fanatic" is now modern society's supreme insult—especially when combined with "religious". The other new pejorative F-word is "Fundamentalist".

When the United States government—*our* government—decided that David Koresh was a "fanatic", federal agents went in with guns blazing and well-known results. The explanation given afterward was that he and his group were "Fundamentalists". (Southern Baptists, beware!)

The media now habitually use the two new F-words to describe the moral philosophy of two thousand years of Catholicism and four thousand years of Judaism, when this philosophy differs from that of the modern secular establishment. The conflict almost always arises monomaniacally (fanatically?) over sexual issues: sodomy, abortion, divorce, fornication, contraception—if we could only revoke the Sixth Commandment, the world would beat a path to our door.

We are living amid a war between gods, between Father, Son, and Holy Spirit, on the one hand, and Moloch, Astarte, and Gaia, on the other.

Three key battlefields are already in the hands of the enemy: education, journalism, and entertainment—the three institutions that most form people's minds. Polls show that the moral beliefs of the leaders in these three areas are wildly at odds with, and in "advance" of, those of society at large. ("Advanced" here means advanced decay.)

Why can't those in the secular establishment just live and let live? Why do they have to sneak an antireligious message into nearly every movie, however gratuitous? (See Michael Medved's book *Hollywood vs. America*.) Why do they hate traditional religions?

The most obvious reason is guilt—the same reason crime hates law, roaches hate light, and cavities hate dentists.

A second reason is fear. Deep down, they know they cannot be *sure* there really is no God of justice and righteousness or that they will not ever be judged by this God, or even damned. No one can prove, no one can be certain, however they laugh or sneer, that sin, Judgment, and Hell are fantasies, not facts.

A third reason is envy. Unconsciously, they envy the very thing they hate and denounce as "fanaticism", the thing Kierkegaard called "infinite passion". The modern world, without God, is passionless, grey, dull, "weary, stale, flat, and unprofitable". For if there is no God, no Heaven, no Hell, no Judgment, no absolute good or evil, then there is no object to elicit infinite passion. Evangelicals, Catholics, Jews, and Muslims believe in a God whose will is the absolute good, a God disobedience to Whom is the supreme evil, and therefore they have an infinite passion. They believe, not merely in human "values", but in divine *commandments*. (God did not give Moses the Ten Values.)

Where can the world find infinite passion without God?

The obvious alternative is sex. Sexual passion is modernity's substitute for religious passion. (Freud declared that religion is a substitute for sex, when in fact, for him and millions more, sex is a substitute for religion.) Saint Thomas explains that "man cannot live without joy. That is why one deprived of spiritual joys goes over to carnal pleasures" (ST II–II, 35, 4 ad 2).

We Christians are accused of being "rigid" in our mind (our doctrines and principles) by those who seek this property only in a lower organ. There are ten commandments, not just one, but the modern mind has only one infinite passion and projects its obsession onto the Church, accusing *us* of being fixated on sex. It's like a teenager on drugs complaining to his parents, who gently disapprove once in a blue moon, "You're always harping on that!"

Any addiction blinds the mind, including the addiction to sex. Paul Johnson, in his book *Intellectuals*, and E. Michael Jones, in *Degenerate Moderns*, have documented how most modern ideology came from sexual deviants and their deviance.

Besides "fanatic" and "Fundamentalist", a third anathema is habitually hurled at Catholic, Evangelical, Jewish, and Muslim morality: "simplistic".

This, too, is an envy-word. Just as secularists envy our passion, they envy our knowledge, our certainty, and our clarity. That is why they trash us. How precious it is to know the difference between the straight road and the crooked; to know that there is good and there is evil, there is right and there is wrong, there is a real black and a real white, as well as things that are grey. Chesterton said, "Morality is always terribly complicated—to a man who has lost his principles."

Deep down, even unbelievers know life must be ultimately simple. They come to know this when someone they love is dying. Then, money and fame and even sex cease to matter. Then, the "simplistic" words of Jesus to the complexifying, modern Martha ring true: "Martha, Martha, you are worried about many things. But only one thing is necessary." Only love is eternal (1 Cor 13:8). "In the evening of our life, we will be judged on our love" (Saint John of the Cross).

The saints all have such real personalities because they know this "one thing necessary". Saint Thomas explains the connection: the unity of a living being comes from its final cause, its end or purpose. So if you have a single ultimate good, your life attains the unity of a work of art. Only if you have "one great love" can you be one great person. To be a real person, you must be a fanatic.

The honest motive for this "fanaticism", however, cannot be psychological; it must be theological. God will not let Himself be used as a tool of psychotherapy. Our fanaticism is to be a response to God, not to our own need; it must be a conformity to the nature of objective reality, to the God who *deserves* our "fanaticism". "Be ye holy for I the Lord your God am holy." The by-product will then be wholeness and happiness. Holiness cannot be a means to wholeness; wholeness must be a by-product of holiness.

Such a unity of purpose is necessary not only for wholeness and happiness but even for sanity. The Nazis drove some Jews in Auschwitz insane, not by torture or starvation or brutally hard labor, but by meaningless work: digging a trench one day and filling it up the next. A hard and painful job for a great and good purpose is endurable; meaningless, purposeless work is not. Childbirth can be easier than retirement. The exhausting life of the peasant poor does not kill the spirit; the boredom of the sophisticated rich does.

The two most common and greatest examples of this unity of purpose, this "one great love", this total self-giving, are religion and family. That is why these are the two things that secularists despise and undermine the most. They are envious.

My characterization of modern secularists is not calculated to win friends and influence people. And if the reader is not mad at me yet, he probably will be by the end of the next paragraph. I can only plead: Ask not whether it makes you feel good; ask only whether it is *true*.

Modern man is—by his own admission—in process, changing. It is man's essence to be unstable and dynamic: he must either rise higher than himself or descend lower. If he does not rise to God, he sinks to bestiality. But which beast? I think modern man is becoming reptilian. Three distinctive features of reptiles are: (1) they devour their young; (2) they are cold-blooded; and (3) they conform their body temperature to their environment. Three features of modern secularists are: (1) they kill their unborn children; (2) they judge the warm-blooded to be "fanatics" (for 98.6 seems like a high fever to the cold-blooded); and (3) they have nothing but their ever-changing society to conform to; they are social relativists with no transcendent absolutes.

If I were to stop here, I would probably have done more harm than good. My purpose is *not* to elicit hatred and resentment or fear and despair. It is to prepare us for war.

We are at war, whether we like it or not. We didn't start it; Satan did, in Eden. It is not a war against flesh and blood but against principalities and powers, and it is fought not with guns but with goodness. We are living in a wicked and wimpy society, and we are watching and smelling as it swirls faster and faster down the drain. Perhaps it is too late to save it; no one knows. But we do know that we can save souls— which are infinitely more important and long-lived than society anyway. We can't stop the war, but we can lower the body count.

How? First, we can keep our powder dry, our passion alive, our "fanaticism" burning. Yesterday, Satan's strategy was fire; today it is water. Yesterday, he inflamed fear and cruelty; today, he tempts to sloth and comfort-mongering and "peace, peace when there is no peace". Yesterday, he was spotted around every corner; today, he has persuaded us that he is a myth. Both strategies are effective: if any army vastly overestimates *or* vastly underestimates its enemy, it will lose battles.

The danger today is not the restoration of the Inquisition. The ACLU is half a millennium behind the times. The danger today is the bland leading the bland. We face not fire but fog.

Second, we must clearly distinguish good fanaticism from bad. *All fanaticism is bad but one*: fanaticism for God. Nothing else is infinitely good; nothing else deserves infinite passion. Not sex, not ideology (Left or Right), not even biological life itself. (Ask any martyr.) We must avoid all false fanaticisms—idolatries—to keep our souls virginally pure for God's love alone. For the final thing we were made for, the one thing for which God will never let us go until we do it, the "one thing necessary", is to love God with all our heart and soul and mind and strength. All Heaven's citizens are fanatics.

We must also clearly distinguish holy from unholy fanaticism. Unholy fanaticism is loud and pushy; holy fanaticism is quiet and humble. It's the difference between Madonna and *the* Madonna.

Mary is the model fanatic. Her whole heart was in her simple Yes, her *fiat*, her *islam* to God. That little word opened the door into this world for The Word. The power that came through her "fanaticism" saved and transformed the world. And He can do it again. And again.

We must also not confuse holy fanaticism with *narrowness*. The saints, who were the most "fanatical" and "simplistic", were also the most fascinatingly creative, unpredictable, and original individuals who ever lived. The reason is simple: once you know the one Absolute, you can sit lightly on and play with everything else, even life itself. The saints crack jokes on their deathbeds. Saint Lawrence, while being roasted over a fire, said, "Turn me over, please; I'm not done on the other side yet." One who has not met God could not understand that attitude.

Without God to be fanatic about, you have to absolutize some idol, for man was designed to be a worshipper. Thus, you become addicted to something less than yourself, something that enslaves you; for "you are a slave to whatever you cannot part with that is less than yourself" (George MacDonald). Even freedom can enslave you. C. S. Lewis writes: "I was not born to be free. I was born to adore and to obey." (Did something thrill in your heart when you read that? Why haven't you heard that before from your teachers?)

Third, we should not be surprised to find an increasing tide of vilification, propaganda, censorship, and outright lies in the three secular establishments. We often wrongly take the fifties as our normal baseline and wonder what went wrong. But history shows that the relative tranquility of that decade is abnormal. The physical wars of the forties and the spiritual wars of the sixties are normal. Our times today are normal. Not peaceful, and not good, but normal. God did not promise us a comfortable mansion in this life. He promised the opposite (for example, Jn 16:33; 1 Pet 4:12). This world is not our home, it's our battlefield. We are to "put on the whole armor of God", not pajamas.

Fourth, if we follow all our Commander's battle instructions, we will also do something all the saints did, but something we don't hear about any more today: we will rejoice when we are persecuted and vilified. Today's instruments of persecution are usually made only of ink, not steel. If we can't rejoice in these little verbal slaps, how will we rejoice in imprisonments (Joan Andrews, Jim Cotter) or martyrdoms (Archbishop Romero)? What a privilege to get so close to the Crucified that a bit of His blood spatters on us!

Fifth, just as our war is defensive, not offensive, it must be positive, not negative. We should love goodness with infinite passion, but we should not hate evil with infinite passion. We are ordered to love God with our whole heart; we are not commanded to hate Satan with our whole heart. Hate has never won a soul. The Inquisition converted no one. Our fanaticism must be a fanaticism of love, for God and for His image in our neighbor, especially our enemy. "The way to conquer your enemy is to make him your friend" (Lincoln). We must love the truth infinitely, but not more than we love our enemies who hate it.

Finally, we must be grateful to God for His holy gift of fanaticism. For if we achieve what our enemies accuse us of ("If you were put on trial for being a Christian, would there be enough evidence to convict you?"), it is only by grace. Saint Thérèse said, "Everything is a grace." Saint Augustine said, "Give what You command, then command what You will." When we love God with all our heart, that is His heart in ours. Only He can build the fire that is His own eternal life of *agape*, wherever it is kindled.

But this is not fatalism. He will do it only when He is asked. "Behold, I stand at the door and knock." In the famous painting of Jesus with a lantern knocking on the door (the soul), there is no knob on the outside of the door. Only you can open the creaky door of your soul to this holy Fanatic who wants to make you like unto Him.

Perhaps Islam is growing faster than Christianity in America because Muslims want to be saints more than Christians do.

Chapter Four

A Defense of "Culture Wars"

A Call for Counterrevolution

What's the Problem?

The problem is to "fight the good fight".

Fight? What fight? Are we at war?

Yes, we are at war. And if you aren't aware of that yet, the most important task this chapter can do for you is to alert you to that fact.

The enemy is not people. The enemy is not humans, but dehumanization: the spectacular and unmistakable social, cultural, and above all moral decline and decay that our society has been suffering for decades.

A generation ago, the five most bothersome problems complained about in polled American high schools were:

a. disrespect for property
b. laziness; not doing homework
c. talking and not paying attention in class
d. throwing spitballs
e. leaving doors and windows open

Does this sound like another world? It is. The same poll was retaken a few years ago. The five leading problems in those same high schools now are:

a. fear of violent death; guns and knives in school

    b. rape

    c. drugs

    d. abortion

    e. getting pregnant

The streets are not safe. The schools are not safe. The society is not safe. Not safe physically and not safe morally.

Parents today feel increasingly trapped and helpless. Control over their children's lives and happiness seems to have passed into the hands of an educational elite whose philosophy of life is radically different from that of the parents and is often a moral vacuum.

At stake in this war is the next generation and the future of this country. It is not a war between generations or races or political parties or religions or economic classes. It is a war between good and evil.

If you love your children or your country, you must take sides in this war. Neutrality is not an option in wartime. For "the only thing that is needed for the triumph of evil is that the good do nothing" (Edmund Burke).

There is a wild divergence between the beliefs and values of ordinary people and those of the intellectual elite, or the teaching establishments in our society (journalism, public education, and entertainment). For instance, according to a poll by the secular Wirthlin Agency in Baltimore,

  — while nearly all Americans (more than 90 percent) believe it is wrong to cheat sexually on your spouse, only about half of media people agree;

  — while about half of all Americans attend religious services regularly, only 9 percent of media people do;

  — while 72 percent (80 percent according to other polls) of Americans feel that abortion is somehow a bad thing and should have some restrictions placed on it by law, *only 3 percent* of media people do.

What is being ignored in our education and degraded in

our entertainment are the moral values that every civilized society in history has believed in: things like self-discipline, character, loyalty, family, civility, courtesy, gentlemanliness, womanliness, and the very idea of objective truth and objective values. America was never a society of saints, but moral values were at least honored and taught. Even if they were "honored more in the breach than in the observance", they were still honored. But they are not honored any more.

What can we do?

There *are* answers. But to get from the problem to the answers, we must go through an analysis of the problem. Diagnosis before treatment. The first and most important point is that there *is* a desperately serious problem and a "culture war" going on.

Next, we will target some of the specific "flash points" or battlefields in this moral war.

Then, we will state some essential principles of a solution: the moral basics without which we cannot survive, the principles now being abandoned that we must recover.

Finally, we will define a few concrete, practical steps we can take.

If you agree that America isn't working and want to know why and how to help fix it, please read on.

What Are the Battlefields?

The Family

This is not a good time for the family, the fundamental foundation and building block of all civilization.

In the Unted States, half of all marriages break up, leaving permanent, devastating, and clearly documented scars on children's lives and behavior.

Fundamental attitudes toward children are changing. In all

previous stable societies, children were regarded as a blessing, and childlessness was regarded as a curse. Today, the attitude is often exactly the opposite.

Child abuse, neglect, abandonment, and abortion all have their fundamental origin in this new "philosophy" that gives children *rights* only if those children are *wanted*. Family violence, teen violence, child abuse, and suicide are spiraling spectacularly. Streets, schools, and even homes are no longer safe. Killers now come in all ages, as young as ten. The feeling of hopelessness permeates many urban families and, increasingly, suburban ones too.

Family breakdown is the one empirically observable, statistically documented, conclusively proven cause of *all* other social ills, even economic ills. We need family-friendly laws and government policies that encourage and reward families instead of those that presently often discourage and penalize them.

Societies have survived with very bad political systems and very bad economies, but not without strong families. Families are to society what cells are to a body. The family is the only place most of us learn life's single most important lesson: unselfish love and lifelong commitment.

I strongly recommend reading the most popular article the *Atlantic Monthly* ever published, "Dan Quayle Was Right", by Barbara Whitehead (April 1993). The massive media barrage against Quayle's commonsensical remark that families without fathers, like Murphy Brown's, are not as desirable as families with fathers revealed far more about the media's hangups than about Quayle's.

The traditional idea of the family—father, mother, and children, faithful and committed to each other for life—did not come from Dan Quayle or from fifties' TV sitcoms but from human nature and the God who designed it. We cannot arbitrarily redefine the family as any voluntary association, including that beween two homosexuals. That definition reduces the family to the same kind of thing as a club or a political action committee or an affair.

Education

The present school-age population is the first generation in American history that is less well educated than their parents (even though the *amount* of education keeps increasing). Quantity is displacing quality.

The educational establishment consistently opposes tried-and-true recipes for educational success, like basics (the three Rs) or phonics or Great Books, and pushes experiments that fail, like the "look-say" reading method, condoms to reduce teenage pregnancy (they almost always have done exactly the opposite), and now "outcome-based education", which systematically penalizes excellence and grades students on "politically correct" *feelings*!

The history textbooks have been rewritten to censor out nearly all mention of God and religion. In this revisionist history, the Pilgrims no longer came to America for religious freedom or gave thanks to God at Thanksgiving. Wherever the founding fathers are quoted, their frequent references to God and religion are clipped out. (See Paul Vitz, *Censorship: Evidence of Bias in our Children's Textbooks*.)

Even long-standing texts have been sharply revised to appeal to the left-of-center educational establishment. The *Wall Street Journal* describes the new revision of the "American Nation" civics texts (first published in 1950) as "a big step backward, a case of 'dumbing down' and revisionist folly in search of a larger audience". In these textbooks, we meet Murphy Brown having a baby and learn that "many Americans were abandoning the idea that marriage was necessarily a lifelong commitment."

The Supreme Court has ruled that it is illegal to display the Ten Commandments in public schools. (For children might be religiously influenced; they might even obey them!) Yet the Ten Commandments are chiseled into the façade of the Supreme Court building where this ruling was made!

It is not legal for a school to invoke God at school convocations. But blasphemy—taking God's name in vain—is protected. So it is legal to disobey the Second Commandment, but illegal to obey it.

Bibles may not be used in any public school activity. But condoms are given out freely. The message is very obvious to all the kids; only the "experts" could miss that one.

(By the way, Planned Parenthood itself estimates that among one hundred couples who use condoms, there will be fourteen pregnancies each year. With a nearly 15-percent failure rate against pregnancy and a much higher failure rate against AIDS [whose virus is much smaller and has no "safe" period], condoms are about as effective against AIDS as a twenty-four-chamber gun instead of a six-chamber gun when playing Russian roulette. Yet condoms are touted as "safe sex". That is how highly some educators think of your child's life.)

John Stuart Mill wrote, "Education is too important to be left to the state." Public education is disappearing; state education is replacing it. A truly public school would be in the hands of the public, that is, the parents, first of all. But our public schools today are becoming more and more the ideological instruments of an educational elite who simply do not respect parents or their values. If you doubt this, just try getting some parents together to investigate and question your children's new sex-education program and note the reaction of the educational and media establishments.

The bottom line is: *Whose* schools are they?

The Media

America is an elitist society, a society of two cultures: ordinary people and "the experts". The vast majority of people still believe in:

— family,
— fidelity (for without it families fail),
— morality (which supports fidelity), and
— religion (which supports morality).

But our media establishment incessantly propagandizes against these four things, which they hate and fear. Even polls by the far-left *Los Angeles Times* in 1992 proved the existence of a massive media bias against traditional values, especially families, fidelity, morality, and religion.

Journalists simply do not report publicity contrary to "their side". Any challenge to the Left is labeled "right-wing extremist" or "Religious Right", including positions always labeled moderate in the past. Major newspapers routinely falsify statistics. The number of deaths annually by *illegal* abortions was arbitrarily set at one hundred thousand, when the actual figure was more like two thousand. Numbers at pro-choice marches are doubled; numbers at pro-life marches are halved or ignored. Homosexuals were declared to constitute 10 percent of the population (that figure was constantly quoted), when the actual figure is 2 or 3 percent. Once exposed, the false figures are simply abandoned. Political candidates who are not "politically correct" are ignored until they say something compromising. Language is deliberately slanted as a matter of policy. Any idea at odds with media orthodoxy is labeled "right-wing extremist". (How often have you read the phrase "left-wing extremist"?)

Personal and Economic Freedom and Self-Determination

One of the pervasive complaints of citizens today is that of helplessness. Life is not as good as it used to be, and there seems to be nothing anyone can do about it.

Fewer families feel they can survive on a single income today. For many individuals, the work ethic no longer works: the willingness to work hard no longer guarantees a job or security. For many, America is no longer "the land of opportunity". The middle class feels crushed from both sides. Numbers and percentages on welfare keep increasing. There are more and more single mothers—who are finding it harder and harder to survive. Small independent businesses are going broke, leaving the state or the country, or giving up their independence. We have less and less control over our income.

The problem is not that we're not *rich* enough but that we're not *free* enough. Not free to walk our own streets or trust our institutions. People feel caught in some vague net called "the system" or "the way things are" or "modern society". The feeling is one of a loss of control. America is no longer felt to be *our* country.

Our time with our children is continuously shrinking. Our sense of community is becoming more tenuous, based more on ideology and less on backyards. Parents feel impotence and loss of control over their own families. Ordinary people no longer seem to be controlling the life of this "democracy", which is moving in the direction of an arrogant oligarchy of the "experts" who are not elected by or accountable to the people at large.

Drugs and Violence

Nothing can so quickly and tragically weaken and destroy a family as drugs. Yet only strong families can keep children from drugs. The same is true of violence: violence weakens families, yet only strong families can deal with it.

No one defends drugs or violence. But how can we win the war against them? Many "experts" are saying that the "war on drugs" is definitively lost. Some (on the Right as well as on the Left) are calling for the legalization of drugs, so your teenager can go to the corner store and buy drugs as easily as buying ice cream.

This capitulation is connected to the pervasive feeling of helplessness mentioned earlier, especially in our cities. Helplessness is both a cause and an effect of drug use. When you feel you have nothing to lose, why not do anything?

Violent criminals are turned out on the street to continue their violence. Criminals are commonly defended more conscientiously than their victims. Rape victims are made to suffer more than rapists. The criminal is seen as a victim, a patient rather than an agent. In other words, the prevailing legal philosophy is a simple, shocking denial of individual moral responsibility.

Removing guns is a poor substitute for removing violent motivation. It changes physical circumstances but does not change minds.

Our society's ability to tolerate violence is a symptom of a deep, underlying moral disease: moral insensitivity. We have become desensitized. Much of the violence and crime begins as early as cartoons, video games, and kids' toys, which teach force as the way to deal with conflict. We are not surprised when a teenager, who has typically seen fifteen thousand murders, rapes, and brutal beatings on TV and MTV and has heard this type of behavior encouraged and idealized on rap "music", turns to violence.

We need to recapture moral outrage. Outrage is the only appropriate response to the outrageous. Mild disgust and disapproval are not enough.

It's time to take back our cities, our streets, our schools, and our children. It's time to draw a line in the sand and say "Enough!"

Abortion

Even people who identify themselves as "pro-choice", like President Clinton, say they want to reduce the number of abortions. This means they, too, assume abortion is bad, for no one wants to reduce the number of something *good*. Surely the deliberate killing of unborn children is not something *good*!

Most Americans will not deny that abortion is at least a moral tragedy. But it is more than that. It is a barbaric act that degrades a civilization.

Polls repeatedly show that the majority of Americans are ignorant of *the basic facts* about abortion:

— the stages of development of life in the womb: just what it is that is aborted;

— the biological and medical facts about just how an abortion is performed. You can see absolutely anything today on TV or MTV or HBO *except* the most frequent medical procedure in America. There is a total media censorship of the facts;

— the numbers: more than one and a half *million* abortions per year. One out of every three children conceived in the United States is aborted;

— the fact that *Roe v. Wade* did *not* restrict abortions, but any woman in America can get an abortion for any reason at all (including sex selection: wanting a son, therefore aborting a daughter) at any time whatsoever;

— the fact that abortion clinics are not legally subject to the same stringent standards of sanitation and safety as all other medical facilities;

— that the anti-abortion movement is much larger than the civil rights movement of the sixties ever was, in numbers of participants and numbers jailed, but the media simply black out these facts;

— that an overwhelming number of women who have had abortions say they regret it later and wish they had not done so;

— that post-abortion trauma is common and crushing; that most women who abort—by their own admission—do *not* believe their "fetus" was "only tissue" or "only potential life" but believe they killed their baby; and this sense of guilt haunts them for life if not dealt with. But this fact is also denied or censored by a total media blackout.

Abortion splits the family in a literal and lethal way. It literally rips mother and child apart. And it desensitizes us in a gruesome way. We are starting to see the next stage in our "culture of death"—legalized suicide and euthanasia. The same principle that justifies killing at one end of life justifies it at the other: *we will dispose of unwanted people.*

The Sexuality of Children

In some cities, half of the *ten*-year-olds are sexually active. Meanwhile, sex education programs that promote abstinence are banned by federal judges for being "religious" (even if they never mention God or religion)! Almost no one *dares* to talk about "sexual purity" any more. Yet it is a medical fact that the only really safe-sex guarantee against AIDS (that is, death) is abstinence before marriage and fidelity afterward. Have we come to the point where teaching virtue is illegal and only deadly vice is legally protected?

We *have* come to the point where sexual virtue is no longer merely a matter of propriety or social acceptability; it is today a matter of physical and psychological survival,

especially for the vastly increasing numbers of children who
are sexually abused and for women who are abandoned,
beaten, or raped by men living the "sexual revolution". We
need a counterrevolution.

We do not need a return to "Victorianism". Nor do we
need to be opposed to sex education in principle, but we do
need to oppose the idea that sex be exempt from the moral
rules we admit in all other areas of life—rules about not
harming other people, keeping promises, and controlling our
instincts. (What other instinct is ever given an absolute right
to self-expression?)

We need once again to agree with Moses, Jesus, Muhammad, Confucius, and all stable and successful societies in
history that sex belongs with marriage, monogamy, and fidelity; that sex is for life, not just for fun; that the taming of the
sex drive and harnessing it to the family are a necessary con-
dition for social stability and long-term human happiness.
The alternative is the chaos we see around us, nearly all directly traceable to family breakdown and the "sexual revolution", that is, sex for exploitation and the "liberal" hypocrisy
that forces all who can't afford private schools to send their
children to state schools to be systematically seduced into losing their morals.

Too many modern educators see the sexuality of children
as a right and parents as impediments to children enjoying
that right. Moreover, they zealously believe that the state
must supersede parents in sensitizing children to sexual practices and behaviors. Parents don't realize the extent to which
this has become an ideological battle.

Parents don't know how bad things have gotten in the
schools because school officials don't allow them to find out.
And the media will not print the pornography that is often
taught under the heading of "sex education" even when discovered and documented by parents.

Moral Principles and Society

Solomon said, "Where there is no vision, the people perish" (Prov 29:18). What is most lacking today is a good vision of the good life. If we had a morally sane philosophy of life, we could see how all our social ills are linked together by the fundamental flaw of a skeptical, cynical, selfish, and materialistic world-and-life-view.

For instance, the common principle behind child abuse, violent crime, and abortion is the principle of responding to problems by violence. Whether in the home, on the streets, or in the womb, violence is violence.

The common principle behind absentee fathers, the breakdown of families, the 50-percent divorce rate, the spread of AIDS, teenage abortions, and giving kids condoms as a cure-all is the principle that unrestricted sex is our one absolute right, regardless of human consequences. The philosophy that sees sex as a commodity to be spent at will really confuses sex with money.

The common principle behind abortion, the distribution of condoms, and the release of rapists is a denial of individual moral responsibility. Abortion means refusing to be responsible for your unborn children. Distributing condoms means young people are not *expected* to be responsible for their sexual behavior—they can say No to smoking or drugs but not to sex. And releasing rapists means seeing "society", not criminals, as responsible for crime.

It is wrong to be judgmental as regards *persons*, but it is equally wrong to refuse to judge *actions*. Otherwise, such a moral relativism is an infallible prescription for social chaos. We must stand for all human beings, but we must stand against dehumanizing deeds.

To make a better society, we need better policies and plans, but these in turn must be based on better principles. Here is a set of very old principles that has worked in the past. Here is a set of ten statements that summarize what Jews, Christians, and Muslims—and rational pagans like Socrates, Aristotle, and Cicero—have always believed about morality.

They are not a Ten Commandments, a specific set of laws. They are about the *status* of moral laws. The specific *content* of moral law is a matter of wide agreement between nearly all cultures and all religions. Justice, charity, self-control, wisdom, courage, loyalty, honesty, and responsibility are universally praised; and injustice, hatred, violence, foolishness, cowardice, betrayal, lying, lust, greed, and irresponsibility are universally blamed—at least they have been until recently. (After all, lust, greed, and irresponsibility sell products very effectively. An addict has little sales resistance.)

The following statements about morality would be enthusiastically embraced by Moses, Solomon, Jesus, Muhammad, Socrates, Confucius, Ghandi, and Buddha, as well as by George Washington, Benjamin Franklin, Thomas Jefferson, and Abraham Lincoln.

1. Morality is *necessary* for society to survive. The alternative is barbarism, decadence, and chaos.

2. Morality is *not sectarian* (religiously) or *partisan* (politically). It is both universally known and universally binding. We all know in our hearts what good and evil are, and we are all responsible for living the way we know we ought to live.

3. Morality is *natural*, or based on human nature. There is a "Natural (moral) Law". Morality is discovered, like stars, not invented, like games. It is not man-made, arbitrary, and changeable. Its laws are intrinsic to human nature, as the laws of hygiene are to the nature of the body or the laws of physics are to the nature of matter.

4. Morality is *liberating, not repressive*. For it is a set of directions given for the purpose of making our human nature

flourish and helping us to reach our full potential. A law like "don't drink poison" is not repressive to your health. Poison is.

5. Morality *takes effort*. Like love, morality is work, not feeling. It is a fight against the forces of evil in all of us. Today it has become a fight against forces in our culture.

6. Morality *gives meaning and purpose and direction to life*. It is a road map. Without a map, we wander aimlessly, hopelessly.

7. Morality *gives human beings dignity*. Its basis is the intrinsic value of the human person. It commands us to love people and use things, not use people and love things. People are ends, things are means.

8. Morality is *reasonable*. It is not blind but intelligent. It perceives a real difference between good and bad actions and lifestyles. It "discriminates". (Discrimination between people as good or bad may be foolish, but discrimination between acts as good or bad is simply moral sanity.) We are a nation born in a struggle for freedom, so we continue to value personal freedom very highly, and rightly so. But *we cannot have freedom without truth*. A surgeon cannot free you from a disease without light to operate by, accurate X rays, and a knowledge of anatomy. Moral skepticism is the death of freedom.

9. Morality is not simply about "freedoms" and "rights" but about *duties and responsibilities*. Victor Frankl says the Statue of Liberty on the East Coast should be completed by a Statue of Responsibility on the West.

10. Morality is *not legalistic*. Its essence is not a set of rules but a vision of the good life and the good person; not only *laws* but also *character*. No set of rules will work without personal virtues. Morality is about how we can be real heroes. It's about how to avoid flunking Life despite getting A's in all your courses.

What Can We Do?

What can we do to win this war?

Much.

We *can* take back our country and our families. We are the majority. There is no reason we must sit back and be cowed by the minority of establishment "experts". We can turn the tide of decadence in America.

How?

Two things are needed: attitudes and actions. Actions alone are not enough; attitudes come first. Doing all the right things with the wrong attitude is self-destructive. So the first thing is to take stock of our *attitudes*. For the spirit in which we act will stamp itself on all our actions and their results.

1. We must *not despair*. Social decay is not inevitable. We are not machines; we *make* machines and fix them. We can fix America for the same reason we made it: because we are free human beings, not helpless machines. And we can fix it by the same moral principles by which we designed it more than three centuries ago.

We must believe that the war *can* be won. We are not pessimists. The tide may already be turning. Ordinary people are now coming to the point of saying "Enough!" For instance, "mere" parents in New York successfully stopped the largest public school bureaucracy in America from imposing its new curriculum of propaganda for sodomy on first-graders ("Daddy's [Gay] Roommate" and "Heather Has Two [Lesbian] Mommies"), despite school board outrage at parental "interference".

2. We must *stop trusting the "experts"*. America is not a nation of experts, by the experts, and for the experts; it is a nation of the people, by the people, and for the people. Our children are not some educator's guinea pigs. Our money does not belong first to the state. We work for ourselves and

our families, not for the System or the Party. We must resolve, by a deliberate decision of mind and will, to return control to the people, where it belongs.

3. We must *love, not hate.* Even if hurt and frustrated, we must not hate, because hate makes only more frustration and hurt. Love alone heals.

We must love our country, which is hurting. We must love our friends and families, who are hurting. That must be our motive for action. If it is, we will win; if it is not, we will lose.

What action?

Individuals and families should pick one specific area they care about most, then get concretely involved in it. Here are some basic ways to do it:

1. *Become informed.* Find out more about what's going on in your schools, in your town, and in your country. In a democracy, those who are uninformed are powerless.

2. *Become involved.* Join support organizations—or start one. Join the front lines. Participate in positive social change. Make it happen! It's not up to the state to make a society what it should be, it's up to the people.

3. *Become vocal.* Talk to your friends and neighbors. Write letters to your newspaper. Contribute to newsletters and church bulletins. For any movement, the pen is the first weapon.

4. *Set an example.* Behave in a way that the world can follow.

5. *Give what you can of yourself* to a good organization or movement that is "fighting the good fight". You can give two precious things: your money and your time. Time for letter writing, or envelope stuffing and addressing, time for organizing and recruiting, or simply time for "talking up" the organization to many friends. It will take sacrifice and suffering. It will mean being sneered at. For some, it may mean being sued, perhaps even jailed, for doing good deeds.

6. *Pray.* Prayer is the most powerful force in the universe. Pray about this sincerely, not just as a nice little psychological trick to make yourself feel good, but to ask God for real power and guidance and (above all) goodness so that you and your society can follow the scriptural command to "Be holy, for I the Lord your God am holy." Ask God to lead you to find what, *specifically*, you can do and whom you can pray for. "More things are wrought by prayer than this world dreams of."

It's up to us.

Chapter Five

Learning from Other Religions

Having defended the *jihad* in "ecumenical jihad" (in Chapters 2, 3, and 4), we now defend the *ecumenical* (in Chapters 5, 6, 7, and 8).

Since Christian ecumenism is an "in-house" affair, so to speak, the point of view changes from an appeal to all men and women of good will to an appeal to Christians, especially Catholics.

We are instructed, by the highest authority in our own Church—an ecumenical council (Vatican II)—that we can and should investigate and learn from the wisdom in other religions. We are also instructed that we should not do that out of any sense of weakness or incompleteness in our own religion, which is the invention not of man but of God. Rather, we should study the teachings of other religions in the same spirit in which the Church Fathers and the medieval Scholastic philosophers, especially Saint Thomas, studied and used the pagan philosophers. Saint Thomas summarized Saint Augustine's principle in using Plato (which was the same principle *he* held in using Aristotle) in the most simple and perfect way possible when he said: "When Augustine, who was imbued with the teachings of the Platonists, found anything therein that was compatible with the [Catholic] faith, he used it; and whenever he found anything incompatible with the faith, he amended it" (ST I, 84, 5).

The result of this open-minded yet critical attitude was the rich synthesis, or marriage, of faith and reason that we know as Christian philosophy. Today the same principle and the same promise apply to our attitude toward other *religions*. For *philosophy* is no longer as influential as it was in ancient or medieval times, but religion is, everywhere in the world except in our own secular Western culture.

There were two other attitudes among Christians toward pagan philosophy in the past, which proved wrong in practice: uncritical rejection and uncritical acceptance. Many Christian writers who thoughtlessly rejected all non-Christian writers as dangerous to the faith eventually became heretics themselves and left the Church (for example, Tatian, Tertullian, and Luther).

If your faith is confident and robust, you can bring together your own Christian faith and non-Christian wisdoms without the fear that your faith might somehow lose in comparison. If you are sure of the truth of your faith, you welcome comparisons, confident beforehand that nothing can threaten your own. For "all truth is God's truth", and therefore all teachings you find in other philosophies or religions (or science, or anywhere else) are either (1) true, and therefore compatible with and not threatening to the truths of Christianity, since truth can never contradict truth; or (2) false, and inferior to Christian truth, and thus once again not threatening to Christian truth.

However, there is also an opposite danger. You can be overbold as well as overcareful. The enthusiasm that comes from discovering something valuable that is new to you can blind you to the need to balance it with other truths. The whole truth, as Christian revelation gives it to us, is full of paradoxes: divine transcendence and divine immanence, human free will and divine sovereignty, God's oneness and God's threeness, Christ's divinity and Christ's humanity, justice and mercy, objective law and subjective motive. When we find in some other religion a deep insight into one truth, it will usually lack the balanced opposite insight that we find in the complete, and therefore paradoxical, Christian revelation. For instance, Islam has a profound insight into God's transcendence and sovereignty but less of a sense of His immanence or intimacy (and no Incarnation, of course). Hinduism, on the other hand, has a profound sense of the divine immanence, or omnipresence, but a questionable sense of His transcendence.

Yet other religions can powerfully remind us of some of the forgotten riches in our tradition. For instance, Oriental concentration on mystical experience should send us to our own mystics. When there are neglected diamonds in our own backyard, it is good to be reminded of them by discovering some in the neighbor's yard.

Religious truth is meant to be lived. Religion is to be studied not as a scientist would study some exotic animal but as you would study your beloved or your family. Religion, unlike science, can be known only from the inside—like a person. That does not mean that you can't understand anything useful or profound about Hinduism without being a Hindu; but it means that you must approach it experientially, at least imagining what it would be like to believe it and live it yourself. When you observe ants in an anthill, you do not try to imagine yourself as one of them. The scientific attitude is quite properly detached, impersonal, and objective. But when you try to understand why your friend is behaving so strangely, you must try to imagine yourself in his skin looking out, you cannot remain outside, looking in.

You must also *do* something about religion. A mere "interest" in religion, as in a kind of fascinating myth on a Joseph

Campbell TV spot, is not religion. Religion involves your life, your time, your lifetime, your blood (that is, your sacrifice). Anything worth doing is worth sacrificing something for.

I have studied and taught and wondered about "comparative religions" for over thirty years, and one of my surest convictions about this subject is that whatever is the real truth about the truth in different religions—that is, whatever God thinks about the different religions of the world—that truth would surprise nearly everyone. *Nobody* yet has a really adequate answer to this fundamental question about the truth in different religions (or perhaps ever will); and the two camps who, I am confident, most certainly do not have the answer are precisely the two who most confidently and certainly claim to have it. These two camps are:

1. those who are sure that all the religions of the world are one and the same deep down; and

2. those who are sure that all the religions of the world are rivals and exclusive and that, if any one is true, each of the others must be fundamentally false at its core.

These two positions are usually given political labels: Left vs. Right, or Liberal vs. Conservative. This habit of labeling illuminates something about the obsession of the labelers, but little or nothing about the things labeled.

Position 1 above amounts to Hinduism; for Hinduism teaches that there is no such thing as error, only lesser truths, lesser "levels of consciousness". So the position that says that all religions are one actually says that all religions are Hinduism on various inferior levels. In other words, Christianity and Hinduism are the same thing, especially Hinduism.

Position 2 really amounts to a denial of one of the teachings of the New Testament and of the Catholic Church: that God "has not left Himself without witness" in the pagan world. (See Romans 1.) This position often gets hung up on words—for instance, Islam's word for God ("Allah") is different from Christianity's, so some Christians think Allah must be a false God, even though all the attributes of the divine nature are the same for Muslims and Christians. (This is not the case for Hindus and Christians; Brahman and God have some attributes that are different and some that are the same.)

The Holy Spirit seems to be working in other religions. There is only one Holy Spirit, and He is the Spirit of Truth, never of error. In studying His works, we are not studying something foreign and threatening, we are studying the Spirit and works of God, whenever His breath blows.

The following chapter will explore some of the precious religious gems of wisdom that we as Christians can rediscover and profit from by studying other religions. One of the great things about religion is that it is free. These gems are for everyone. Unlike physical goods, they do not diminish when shared. There is no need for any competition. There is plenty of truth to go around.

Chapter Six

What Christians Can Learn from Confucius, Buddha, Muhammad, and Moses

There has been a last-minute change. The chapter I had originally planned to write has been lost. No, not lost, thrown away. I dumped it in the wastebasket. Why? Because, as I was planning it, something that you will probably not believe happened to me. But I have to tell you about it anyway. I am *commanded* to tell you. Woe is me if I do not preach this gospel.

You've all heard about OBEs, out-of-body experiences, in which a person's soul leaves his body and sometimes seems to experience some foretaste of Heaven. Well, it happened to me.

It usually happens when something mystical triggers it: most usually imminent death, or the expectation of death, or something so ecstatic that you lose self-consciousness. Well, I was engrossed in the most mystical thing I know on earth: surfing. Hurricane Felix had turned the East Coast into Hawaii for two weeks, and I wanted to catch a piece of the action. I was paddling out to catch a twelve-foot wave when *it* caught *me*, and broke over me like a giant cobra. I'm a clumsy Dutchman; I shouldn't try to ride stallion waves, only pony waves. I thought to myself: You are now about to drown. Yet I was not afraid. I had no time to be afraid. For in that split second, before I wiped out, my mind left my body and experienced something I will now reveal to you. Whether what I experienced was Heaven or earth, I cannot say. Whether it was real or unreal, objective truth or subjective fantasy, I cannot say. All I can say is that it was certainly truer, incomparably truer, than the chapter I was planning to write. That's why I threw the old one away.

The tunnel of water, the wave that demolished me, became a tunnel of light. I soul-surfed the wave of light and landed on a Heavenly beach, where the very sand was made of golden light. Suddenly I saw a man walking toward me down the beach. He had a serene smile on his face. He looked just like the pictures of Confucius that I had seen in books, except for the surfboard he was carrying. (But I figured it was natural for everyone to be a surfer in Heaven.) If this was Confucius, our meeting was providential, since I had planned to begin this chapter by suggesting that Christians should learn from Confucius something about the central importance of social justice, the importance of the Social Gospel, the fact that building a just society here on earth is not some secular addition to the gospel but an essential aspect of the gospel itself.

But Confucius seemed to know me and to know my thoughts and plans before I spoke or wrote them. Without introducing himself, he immediately plunged into his style of teaching by questioning.

He asked me, "Would you rather teach these people, or not?"

"Teach, of course", I replied.

"And are teaching and learning correlative?"

"Yes", I said.

"So you teach if and only if they learn?"

"Yes", I said again, wondering now whether this was Confucius or Socrates in disguise.

He went on: "And can they learn what they already know or what they do not yet know?"

"What they do not yet know", I answered.

"And do your readers not know that the gospel is social? Are they hermits? Are they mystics? Are they Fundamentalists?"

"No", I said.

"Then why do you try to teach them what they already know?"

I had no answer. But he would not drop his questioning. "It could not be for *their* sake, for their improvement, so it must be for your own, to curry their favor, to become popular."

I could not lie in the presence of this light. "You are right", I said. "But then what can I tell them?"

"Do you really want to learn from me something to tell them?" he asked, looking me straight in the eye.

"Yes", I said.

"About what?"

"About society and social justice."

"Good. Because I really know something about that. The most successful and stable society in all of human history was based on my teachings, and it worked in the most populous country on earth."

"That's right", I remembered, "Confucian China lasted well over two thousand years—three times longer than Rome, ten times longer than America. It really worked. How did you do it?"

"Well, now," smiled Confucius, "you're finally asking the right question. Thank you."

"And would you perhaps oblige me by setting aside your dialogue method for a minute and giving me some answers instead of asking me questions?" I made bold to ask.

"I will try", he said.

"So what can you teach me?"

He smiled. "The title of your chapter, I believe, is what Christians can *learn* from non–Christian religions. If you really want to learn, here's what I can teach.

"I lived in a time called 'the Period of Warring States'. China had been racked with civil and dynastic wars for generations. So I first diagnosed the cause of the disease, like a doctor probing beneath the symptoms. What is the source of war? I asked. And the answer seemed obvious from experience and observation. War always stems from greed, from selfishness, from self-assertion."

He noted my nod of approval and went on.

"Next, I asked how we can treat this disease. I realized that appeals to *individuals* to act unselfishly were not sufficient to overcome that strong inner force (which you Christians know as 'Original Sin'); I realized that social sanctions and social structures were also needed to channel it and tame it, like sandbagging a flooding river. So I taught an elaborate system of social structures and rules, somewhat similar in spirit to Orthodox Judaism, though not as explicitly religious. In such a society the individual could find fulfillment and happiness only in right relationships, especially family relationships. These, in turn, could be successful only through the practice of the natural virtues as I defined them —a very common and noncontroversial list . . ."

"I know the list", I interrupted, to save time.

"Good. And I hope you also know the single fundamental core of all of them."

"What's that?"

"Harmony", he answered.

"Not justice?" I asked.

"Social justice *means* harmony", he answered. "The two are not alternatives. Justice is like music."

"What do you mean by that? How do you secure each individual's rights?"

"Justice isn't a matter of balancing individual rights. It's not negotiating different self-assertions. It's fitting into the cosmic order. Your notion of justice as asserting individual rights only *undermines* justice and leads to envy, resentment, and competition. Instead, you must subordinate yourself to the whole, to the social order that in turn is a mirror of the cosmic order—what I called 'the will of heaven' and what you used to call the 'Natural Law'. Only when you subordinate yourself will you find yourself—as one of your own prophets has said." He looked at me with a kind of gentle sarcasm.

"Wait", I interrupted. "What you said about rights shocks me. How can you ignore rights?"

"I answer your question with another question. Who is it that ignores rights? What kind of people never speak about their rights?"

"I don't know. You tell me."

His one-word answer floored me: "Lovers. Does not your own religion teach you that love is the supreme value?"

I had no answer to this. He went on:

"Justice is not equality. It's like music: harmony among unequal instruments, each in its proper place, each needed but each subordinating itself to the whole. And since justice is not equality, do *not* treat everyone equally. Justice means treating equals equally *and unequals unequally*. Old and young, men and women, parents and children, older brother and younger brother, older sister and younger sister, older brother and older sister—different scores for each instrument. As one of your own theologians has written, 'Truth is symphonic.'"

"And will this politics of harmony save society?" I asked.

"Politics can't save society. Only virtue can. You have to be a moralist. And society has to teach this moralism repeatedly.

Everyone must be totally immersed in it—both in public and in private, in the state and in the school and in the home, by books and by living examples, by constant repetition. It's just what you're taught in your own Scriptures. Don't look surprised. Didn't you ever read Deuteronomy 6 and 11?"

I must have looked embarrassed, for he went on: "The very things your educational establishment is most embarrassed at—moralizing, virtue-talk, tradition, authority, self-discipline, self-abnegation, conformity, humility—all this is the very secret of my success, the lasting power of my social revolution."

"What about individual freedom? What if I don't want to keep hearing moral lessons? What of my rights—?"

He interrupted me with a sad side-to-side headshake. "Moral goodness is much more important than freedom or rights, shocking as that may sound to you. Only virtuous people will be free, and only virtuous people will freely grant each other their rights. So virtue is the practical foundation of both rights and freedoms, not vice versa."

"Is this *individual*, private virtue or *social*, public virtue that you are putting first?" I asked.

"Something between the two, which is the foundation for both."

"What could that possibly be?"

"The family. How could you have forgotten it? Only good families can make good states; isolated, uprooted individualists can't. And only good families can teach individuals to be good. The state can't. So 'family values' must come first. And these families must be enlarged, not shrunk—in size as well as importance. Large extended families work. Murphy Brown does not."

"But . . . " I stammered. "You sound like . . . like. . . . " I could not bring myself to say the dreaded word, the Q-word. He said it for me.

"Like Dan Quayle?"

"Yes," I wailed, "like Dan Quayle!"

"Why does the name when it comes out of your mouth sound like something between a joke and a disease?"

"Because this man can't even spell 'potato' ", I blurted out.

"Is spelling what makes a man wise?" he asked.

"No, but he's not very bright or original or creative or progressive . . . and now I'm beginning to think of you in the same way: as a sort of Asian Forrest Gump."

"Thank you for the compliment", he said.

"I didn't mean it as a compliment", I protested.

"But I take it as one", he replied, and added, "You see, simple, ordinary, populist, familiar, familial, conservative common sense *works*. And everyone knows that *except* your experts and professional educators. So tell them. Tell them what they've forgotten. Tell them the old platitudes, the truisms, the things I taught, the things that are so obvious that teaching them made me the most boring teacher in history— and the most successful. Tell them about the goodness of goodness and the badness of badness. That's Lesson One, and your society is dying because you've forgotten it or doubted it or denied it or fudged it or fuzzied it or 'nuanced' it. You can't build on any other foundation. And that's what you're trying to do: to build a skyscraper on sand. Remember: tell them what they've forgotten, not what they've remembered. After all, you at least pretended in your title that you wanted to *learn* from other religions. Well, here's what mine has to teach you. Take it, and find a culture of peace and life, or leave it, as you are doing, and find a culture of chaos and death."

At that, Confucius suddenly disappeared. I had no time to ponder his wisdom or to wonder about his disappearance, for immediately a second man appeared, much larger and fatter but also with Oriental features. "Buddha?" I guessed. An inscrutable smile was his only answer; then he offered me a lotus flower, and I knew my guess was right. "Will you also offer me your wisdom in words as well as in flowers?" I asked. To my surprise, he answered, "Yes", and I smiled with expectation. I expected him to say something about the ineffability of truth or the ultimate oneness of all things or true religion's transcendence of all forms and concepts—themes I had planned to include in my chapter about what Christians should learn from other religions. Instead, he said the following:

"I will speak plainly rather than mysteriously to you, because you are very obtuse. I have heard what my brother Confucius has told you. I do not disagree with what he said, but I add to it. Confucius has told you what you may call, in terms from your Scripture, the wisdom of Martha. I tell you the wisdom of Mary. [From this scriptural reference I concluded that Buddha had had a theological crash course somewhere in Heaven.] And I, like he, tell you not what you have remembered but what you have forgotten. What you have forgotten, especially in America, is that Martha without Mary has missed 'the one thing necessary', the only thing absolutely necessary. She has grasped after and worried over the ten thousand things under the sun and has refused to let them drop from her hand even for a sacred second, as Mary did. Thus, in remembering the ten thousand, she has forgotten the one, the one thing needful. And that thing is not justice or the good society or good deeds or ethics or politics or anything you can do. It is one of your classic American superstitions that you can solve every problem by *doing* something about it. [I opened my eyes and my mind wide at this point.] Your own Scriptures tell you differently. The deepest problems of all can be solved only by *receiving*, not doing. As a very good friend of mine, Lao-Tzu, has put it, you must learn the art of *wei-wu-wei*, 'doing by not doing'. Most people in your society have unlearned that old wisdom, a wisdom shared by Buddhist and Christian saints alike. Your parishes are beehives of Martha-like activism—programs and organizations and conferences and meetings and planning and fund-raising and busy, fussy do-gooding. You are still walking down the road that produced the early Luther: the road of works-righteousness, of do-it-yourself salvation— the old Pelagian heresy in new American dress. It is leading your culture to stress, guilt, breakdown, depression, and violence. Why do you let yourself be led by this culture instead of leading it?"

I was surprised that Buddha was talking to me in such direct and nonmystical terms. But I did not complain about his clarity. Instead, I let my reason question him: "You say you do not disagree with Confucius. Yet you seem to do just that by calling him Martha the activist and yourself Mary the contemplative."

"There is no disagreement", he said. "We must do the works of Martha, but in the spirit of Mary. Both of us would agree with that."

"What is the spirit of Mary?" I asked.

"Silence", he said. "Interior silence—and exterior silence too. Your culture cannot hear the voice of God because its ears are too full of noise. For lack of silence you are going mad. God made you with two ears and only one tongue, so that you could listen twice as much as you speak. Then, when words come out of the silence, they will have power. Words that come only out of other words are but the chatter of bureaucrats and scholars presenting papers at conferences."

"But do you deny that social justice is essential?" I asked.

"No", he said. "I deny that it can ever come from any other source than the Spirit." This confirmed my suspicion that Buddha had indeed come from Heaven, since he had spoken of God, of Mary and Martha in the Gospel, and now of the Spirit. He went on: "In fact, Confucius has taught you that, too, in his fundamental formula for social success:

> If there is peace in the heart, there will be peace in the family.
> If there is peace in the family, there will be peace in the city.
> If there is peace in the city, there will be peace in the nation.
> If there is peace in the nation, there will be peace in the world."

"So the first step is to have peace in the heart toward my neighbor?" I asked.

"Have you forgotten your own Scriptures?" he chided me. "The first and greatest commandment is to love *God* with all your heart, to have peace with God. Only then will your love of your neighbor be filled with a more than human power and peace." Again I was startled and heartened to hear Buddha speak of God. He went on: "Did not one of your most popular writers, Thomas Merton, sum up all your social problems in two sentences? 'We are not at peace with each other because we are not at peace with ourselves. And we are not at peace with ourselves because we are not at peace with God.'"

I was impressed with this simple wisdom, but I voiced a worry about it: "Isn't there a danger in focusing all our attention on God instead of on our neighbor?"

"No!" was the reply. "For God will always send you to your neighbor. But your neighbor will not always send you to God. Mary will never supplant Martha, but Martha may supplant Mary. Listening to God will never dull your ear to your neighbor; it will sharpen it."

I was impatient to move beyond this simple lesson and curious about what had happened to Buddha since his death. So I asked, "Are you a Christian now and not a Buddhist?"

In reply, he asked: "What did the Buddha teach? What but the Four Noble Truths? And of the four, which is the crucial one? The second, the diagnosis of all human suffering as stemming from craving, from greed and lust. This teaching remains true, and my alternative, my prescription for a cure, also remains true. In a word, it is what all your saints called *detachment*. Without it there is no liberation from your slavery to time, to clocks, to activism, to your own ego. Your own saints taught you the same thing, or the same three things: cultivate poverty, chastity, and obedience, not money, sex, and power; not the world, the flesh, and the devil; not greed, lust, and pride. These last three groups are the main ingredients of what I called *tanha*, selfish craving, the cause of all your problems. Let them die. Don't feed those beasts food; let them die. Then God can be born in you. This is your *wei-wu-wei*. Let your souls be wombs, be women, be anima, be open, be tubes for the wind of God's Spirit to blow through you, in one end and out the other, in by contemplation and out by action, in by faith and out by works, in by Mary and out by Martha."

I was dwarfed by this mountain of wisdom and knew not what to say, except to ask a foolish question, to which Buddha gave a very unfoolish answer. "That sounds like a wonderful sermon, but can you be more specific and practical?"

"Yes", he said, with an "all right, sucker, you asked for it" smile. "Here are some specifics. Be sure you pray two hours for each hour you speak. And when you pray, be sure you listen to two of God's words for every one of your own that you speak. I have already spoken far more words than I would have liked."

"I wondered about that", I asked. "Why this change of style, from mystic to prophet?"

"Because I practiced what I preach", he replied. "When I got here—yes, we are in the outskirts of Heaven, the place you call Purgatory—I listened, and God spoke. He commanded, and I obeyed. The change of style is His idea, not mine. I am His prophet now."

"Then I am encouraged to ask you a direct and honest question", I said. "This 'one thing necessary' stuff, this concentration on silence and prayer and reception—isn't it one-sided? Exaggerated? Overdone?"

He replied, with a stern face: "When I was on earth, I did not know God, nor did I claim to. Yet I knew more about what was owed to Him than you do, despite all your religious training, it seems, to judge from your foolish question. I knew even then that there was something—I called it Enlightenment, or Nirvana—that was infinitely more important than life itself, far more than 'a matter of life or death'. The true Buddhist would willingly risk or sacrifice anything and everything for this. He knows that if he does not attain it, his life is truly a failure even if it contains every imaginable earthly success, and that if he does attain it, his life is truly a success even if it contains every imaginable earthly failure. Thus he sometimes performs extremely arduous and bizarre tasks given to him by his spiritual master, or *roshi*, in the hope that these will lead to Enlightenment: tasks like spending years in a monastery doing nothing but washing dishes, or spending fourteen hours a day staring at a wall, or struggling with an insoluble *koan* puzzle night and day for a lifetime. The disciple does these things only because he totally trusts the *roshi* and only because he knows that it does not profit a man to gain the whole world and lose his Enlightenment. Do you not also have a *roshi* who told you that? One wiser than any Buddhist *roshi*, and infinitely wiser than I? Did He not command you to be a crazy fanatic and to sell all that you had for this one 'pearl of great price'? Have you not shied away from this teaching as socially unacceptable in your bored, cynical, and sophisticated society? Is that not why life is so dull and empty today? Why it lacks an edge, a knife, an absolute?"

"You mean my *roshi* is Christ?"

"Of course!" he retorted. "A Buddhist *roshi* works with his disciples only a few minutes or a few hours a day, and usually in groups, but you have God Himself as your *roshi,* taking personal charge of your individual instruction every second of every day, guiding you through all the events of your life. Every wart and every war, every cancer and every piece of candy, the fall of every hair from your head and every sparrow from the sky—all are perfectly planned and provided, tailored like a custom-made coat—for what end? For nothing? For obedience to the law of gravity? Do you think He cares more about gravity than about grace? It is all for *you*, for your instruction. He created the whole universe for you, for your eternal soul, for your Heaven. I did not know either Him or the soul or Heaven, but I knew that there had to be just one thing that everything was for, everything was about. And you, who know God and the soul and Heaven—how can you have forgotten this?"

Buddha then condescended to my love of logic and reasoned with me: "If this is not true, then there are only five possibilities: (1) there is no divine *roshi* at all, no God; or (2) He is not present to your life, providentially directing you, but is absent and unconcerned; or (3) He is weak and has not "got the whole world in His hands"; or (4) He is wicked or selfish and does not love you or care for you; or (5) He is stupid and makes mistakes in guiding you. These are the five essential heresies of (1) atheism, (2) deism, (3) naturalism, (4) pantheism, and (5) paganism, denying God's (1) existence, (2) presence, (3) power, (4) love, or (5) wisdom. The only alternative to these denials is the denial of yourself and your own natural tendency to look at some apparent accident or loss or tragedy in your life as a mistake on the part of your divine *roshi*. Either God is your perfect guide to perfect Enlightenment, or you are adrift in hopeless darkness. And now, what were you saying about my exaggerating?"

I stood shamefaced and answerless. A few more silly questions sprang out of my mind's womb, but they died on my lips. When Buddha saw this, he smiled with satisfaction and disappeared, as Confucius had done, leaving only his inscrutable smile, like the Cheshire cat's, an upside-down rainbow against the sky.

Buddha's serene smile was so contagious that I found myself smiling serenely too and almost slipping into sleep, when I was rudely awakened by a man with a black mustache, flashing black eyes, a red turban, and a curved sword. I did not like the look of him at all, and I silently prayed, "Lord, deliver me from this man." Imagine my surprise when these words formed themselves clearly in my mind: "I will not." I cannot explain to you *how* I knew, but I knew these words were God's.

"Why, Lord?" I asked.

"Because this man will teach you a more important lesson than even Confucius or Buddha."

"What lesson, Lord?"

"He will teach you the heart and soul of all true religion."

I was shocked by this, since the man was evidently Muhammad. I wondered how a man who was not even a Christian could teach me the heart and soul of all true religion. But I could not argue with the Lord. So I asked: "And what is the heart and soul of all true religion?"

The answer came from Muhammad, in a single word. "*Islam*", he said. "*Islam*—surrender—and the peace that comes from surrender, the peace the world cannot give, that comes only from total surrender to the will of God. This is the heart and soul of all true religion. How could you have forgotten? Why does it take an alien to remind you? Have you no saints and prophets of your own?"

I was dumbfounded and knew not what to say to this man, whom I had learned to fear as a violent and dangerous bigot. I blurted out what was in my heart: "Are you indeed Muhammad? And are you truly a prophet? Are your words from God? And is your God the same as our God?"

"Yes, yes, a thousand times yes to all four questions", he said.

"But how can you come as God's prophet to teach me what I already know?" I objected. "Is not the function of a prophet to tell us what we do *not* know?" (You see, by now I had learned at least the first lesson Confucius had taught me.)

"That is true", he said. "But you do *not* know it. If you had learned this lesson, the simplest lesson in the world, you would have peace in your hearts and in your homes and in your streets. God's Kingdom would come, and His will would be done on earth as perfectly and as peacefully as it is done in Heaven, if only you meant it with all your heart when you prayed: '*Thy* name be hallowed, *Thy* Kingdom come, *Thy* will be done.' Because you do not begin there; because you have forgotten the first petition of your first prayer, everything that follows, follows a false first step. The only true first step is adoration, the bent knee and the bent spirit, surrender, *islam*."

This was too scandalously simple for me. I turned the conversation to another point. "Are you a Christian now or a Muslim?"

He gave what seemed to me an evasive answer: "Why do you say 'or'? How can one be a Christian without *islam* to the one God?"

Because I thought his answer evasive, I challenged him

more directly. "If you come from Heaven and not from Hell, what do you say to *this*?" And I whipped out my Rosary and held aloft the crucifix, as I would to Dracula. To my wondering eyes, Muhammad fell to his knees and crossed himself. My response was the only possible one: I bowed the knees of my mind to the words of the man who had bowed his knees to my Lord and His Mother, though his words were not the ones I was expecting.

His words were these: "You are not winning your world, you are not winning your war, your jihad, your spiritual warfare; your world is sliding down the road to Hell. Why? Why have you lost a century to the devil? Not because your scholars are not subtle enough or because your coffers are not full enough or because your numbers are not large enough or because your ideology is not liberal enough or conservative enough, but because you prattle about yourselves and your freedoms and your rights and your self-fulfillment rather than forgetting yourself and adoring and obeying the Lord. That is the only road that can take you to the heights of victory: the low road of submission, *islam*, obedience—a thing so simple a child can understand it: the child you must become again if you are to enter His Kingdom. The saying is His, not mine. I am only His prophet; He is the One than whom there is no other. *La illa ha illa Allah!*" And he fell to his knees and bowed his back and prayed.

The comfortably condescending cultural chauvinism with which I had always unconsciously viewed those holy Arabic words and that holy Arabic deed seemed to have suddenly died in me, and I asked myself whether my own tepid piety might not have had a more proper fire had I bowed my back, my tongue, and my heart as completely as he and his followers had. I wondered also whether my world could ever be saved in any other way. Confucius and Buddha and Muhammad all came together in this thought: that the only

way to change our bad society into a good society like the
one Confucius masterminded was by letting God do it, by
islam, as Muhammad put it; by *wei-wu-wei*, as Buddha's spiritual brother Lao-Tzu put it. I suspected then that the explosive growth of Islam in our time might be due to a simpler
cause than any sociologist has yet discovered: that God blesses
obedience and faithfulness, especially when surrounded by
unfaithful and disobedient cultures. The idea was much too
simple for a scholar to accept. But, I remembered, it was an
idea repeated hundreds of times in the Jewish and Christian
Scriptures. I remembered also that the Chosen People, the
only ones with an infallible, direct, divine revelation in ancient times, the only ones with the pure truth, were less
pleasing to God than many of the Gentiles were, were less
faithful to the light they had, and were threatened with more
severe punishments, both temporal and eternal, by God's
prophets. How could I be sure the same thing could not happen to the Church, the new Israel?

Muhammad went on: "You have forgotten the simple lesson of all your saints. You have become complexified, confused, and compromised, attached to your own divided wills,
your own agendas, and your own desires (which you frequently mislabel your 'needs'); that is why you have lost sight
of the simple fact that is as hard and clear as the desert sun.
The religion I taught my people was the simplest one in the
world. There are times that call for complexity, and there are
times that call for simplicity. Today is a time when 'simplistic'
is the favorite sneer word of a decadent, arrogant, corrupt,
and aggressively anti-God establishment. So what time do
you think it is today?"

I had nothing to say, so Muhammad answered his own
question. "It is time for a jihad, a holy war, a spiritual war.
Rather, it is time to wake up to the fact that, whether you
like it or not, you are in the middle of one."

"But we are commanded to love our enemies, not to make war", I protested.

"We love our human enemies, we war against our spirit enemies", he replied.

"Aren't Muslims famous for confusing the two and fighting literal holy wars?"

"Some", he admitted. "About 5 percent of Muslims in the world believe that the jihad means physical war, killing infidels. But the Qur'an makes it quite clear that this war is first within oneself and against one's own sins and infidelities."

"But your people, the Arabs, are world-famous for violence."

"Unlike your people in Northern Ireland, I suppose."

"But your whole history is full of—"

"Crusades and inquisitions and forced conversions and anti-Semitism and religious wars?" I quickly realized that my "argument" was going nowhere except to blow up in my face.

"Let me try to explain", he said more gently. "*Islam* and jihad are intrinsically connected. For *islam* means not only 'submission' but also 'peace', the peace that the world cannot give, the peace that only God can give, when we submit to Him. And this submission requires the inner jihad, a war on our war against God. So we get the paradoxical result that peace (*islam*) is attained only through war (jihad). And this peace also *leads to* war, because the submission that *is* this peace requires us to obey God's will, and God's will for us is for us to become spiritual warriors against evil."

"I see", I replied. "But aren't those two ideas more appropriate for a simple and primitive time than for today?"

"Exactly the opposite!" he retorted. "You are on a battlefield, and you do not know it. You need a trumpet call to wake you up. God will not save your sick society without your cooperation. And that cooperation can be summarized in the two words *islam* and jihad."

"It sounds so simple . . . ", I protested.

"That's the point", he replied. "It *is* simple. Like the point of an arrow. It will not penetrate if it is well rounded. The way the Lord has laid out for us is what Jesus called 'the *narrow* way' and I called 'the straight path'. Your age is the age of innumerable options, side paths, escapes, excuses, complexifications, and nuancing. To a culture that uses the phrase 'a complex issue' for mothers murdering their unborn babies, Islam comes with the prophetic 'Thus says the Lord!' You Christians have the same word in far greater fullness than my people do, yet you are far more afraid to speak it. We will put you to shame. I am not proud of my mistakes, but I am proud of my people. Their knowledge of salvation is incomparably less than yours, but their hearts are often very close to the heart of God. They have taken the water of simple theism and made it into a heady wine, while you have taken the wine of the fullness of God's revelation and turned it into lukewarm water."

I became a bit defensive and combative at this point. "So you have abjured your Qur'an, then, in embracing our Bible instead?"

To my surprise, Muhammad shouted, "No! How could I abjure a divine revelation?"

"But how could a Christian believe the Qur'an is a divine revelation?" I asked.

"How could he think anything else?" was the reply. "Tell me, what pagan philosopher came the closest to the Scriptures in knowing the true nature of God, do you think?"

"Aristotle, I guess."

"And he had no divine revelation but only human reason."

"Right."

"Now compare the knowledge of God in the Qur'an with

the knowledge of God in Aristotle. If it was my reason, rather than God's revelation, that was responsible for the knowledge of God in the Qur'an, then I was far and away the greatest philosopher who ever lived. I was to Aristotle what Aristotle was to a one-day-old baby."

"But how could the Qur'an be divine revelation? God does not contradict Himself, but the Qur'an contradicts the Bible at some points. How can divine revelation err?"

"It cannot err insofar as it is divine revelation", Muhammad answered. "But it is not the same thing to say it is *revelation* and to say it is *errorless*. The light of God can fall on human windows clouded with fog. Your own Church says the same regarding private revelations."

I had no answer to this, so I tried a new tack, one I had heard from almost all my Protestant friends: "But isn't the God of the Qur'an very different from the God of the Bible?"

"Not at all! Each of the ninety-nine divine attributes mentioned in the Qur'an is also mentioned in the Bible. Even the proportion is the same: His mercy is mentioned ten times more often than His judgment—in both books."

"I did not know that", I confessed. "I had been taught otherwise."

"I suppose you also did not know that the Qur'an attributes no shortcomings of any kind to Jesus. And that it says (3.59) that He was one of only two men who were immediately created by God, rather than having a human father. (The other was Adam.) And that it calls Jesus 'the Word of God' (4.171). And that it says He had the power to work miracles, even giving life to the dead (5.110). And that He shares with the angels the experience of being in God's presence (4.172)."

"But you denied that He is the Son of God! You wrote that it was not fitting for God to have a son."

"I did. But I also wrote (43.81), 'If God Most Gracious had a son, I would be the first to worship.' This was divinely inspired prophecy, for when I entered Heaven I immediately worshipped my Savior, whom I recognized. I hope most of my pious followers will follow this last step of my pilgrimage as well. If they cannot do it on earth, they may still do so in Heaven, as I did."

"There are many Catholics who would be very, very suspicious of this. They say you and your work were from the devil, not from God."

"This is a very serious charge to make", he replied. "When the Pharisees said that the works of Jesus were inspired by the devil, Jesus began to warn them about the 'unforgivable sin'. When you demonize men, demons may take it less lightly than men do."

I must have looked puzzled and uncertain at this point. Muhammad clinched his point by asking: "Is it not true that for orthodox Catholics the surest test of heresy is Mary? No heretic can endure her, nor she them. Now what did I say about Mary in the Qur'an? I mentioned her thirty-four times, more than any other woman. I praised her so effusively that you could call me 'the Marian prophet'. She is the only woman I mentioned by name. I called her 'pure and exalted . . . above womankind' (3.42). And I affirmed that God breathed His Spirit into her and made her virginally born Son a sign to all men (21.91; 66.12). If Mary is the touchstone of Catholic truth, I was closer in spirit to the touchstone than most of your Protestant brethren."

I resolved to have a second look at this man whom I had thought of as an enemy and now was beginning to reconsider as a friend. But I had no time to do or even think, for he faded from my view, to be replaced by still another man.

Muhammad had seemed to tower over me, but he was dwarfed by the figure who next loomed upon my sight as

Muhammad faded away. This new man seemed to have emerged from deep waters yet at the same time to have come down from a great height. In one hand he held some wet bulrushes; in the other, two stone tablets. "Moses?" I asked, half a greeting, half a question. To my amazement, he replied, in a lower East Side New York accent, "You were expecting maybe Santa Claus?"

I blurted out: "But you're so . . . " and stopped, embarrassed.

"So Jewish? So say it, it won't bite! What, I should be a *WASP* or something, now I'm in Heaven?"

"How odd . . . " I murmured, then stopped. Moses finished the quotation for me:

" 'How odd/ of God/ to choose/ the Jews.' Hilaire Belloc, right? One of my favorite writers. A big mouth, like me."

"But I thought he was sort of anti-Semitic", I said.

"Sure, he was a bastard, but hey, he took us seriously at least. None of this patronizing P.C. garbage about multi-culturalism. Better we should get a verbal kick in the pants than a verbal pat on the head. *We are different.* Always were, always will be. How could it not be?—the Lord became a Jew! Not just a man, a Jew. And I think that is still a pretty hard thing for you to digest, am I right?"

"Yes", I replied, unable to speak anything but truth in this country.

"One of your big-mouth authors like myself—Walker Percy, his name is—said it right: Language is so worn out and defaced today that the word 'Jew' is the only word that still has teeth left in it."

"But our problem is not anti-Semitism. It's what theologians call 'the scandal of particularity'."

"Hmph!" Moses snorted. "Better they should call your so-called Enlightenment 'the scandal of universality'."

"What do you mean?" I asked.

"I mean the stupid idea of some generic God, without a place, without a personality, without a people—more like a proposition than a person. Maybe you should worship instead an alligator or something; at least that's real."

"Is this what you have come to teach me? That the scandal of particularity is not a scandal at all?"

"You said it", Moses replied.

"Can you show me how?"

"Look"—he began to reason with me like an uncle— "What's your culture really, really good at? What are you best at?"

"Science and technology, I guess", I answered.

"You guess right", he said. "So what do you think would happen if you treated all scientific theories as equal?"

"That would be stupid", I said, "Science would never get anywhere."

"Right again", he said. "So what's the good word? *Discrimination!* A is right and B is wrong. A is better and B is worse."

"What's your point?" I asked.

"Are your ears full of wax? Didn't you hear me? Discrimination! It's a good idea. You ought to try it some time. God's idea, it was. That's how He created. Don't you remember my poem on the subject? I thought it was kind of famous. But maybe you don't go in for creation stories nowadays? Look, here's how He did it. First he discriminates being from nonbeing, then light from darkness, earth from heavens, land from water, living from nonliving, mammals from fish, man from animal—and then right from wrong, obedience from disobedience, unforbidden from forbidden."

"Well, you know, Moses, I'm an American, and we kind of prefer equality to discrimination."

"You sure do!" he bellowed. "That's why you're going to Hell!"

"What??"

"You heard me. Because you're more afraid of discrimination than you are of Hell, you've let America teach you instead of you teaching her. All that stuff about salt losing its savor—whom do you think He meant to insult there? First-century Jews? No, he was looking down the centuries at twentieth-century American Catholics. That stuff was mailed to your address, bubeleh."

"I think that's a bit unfair . . . "

"Oh, yeah? Look at statistics. You Catholics fornicate at the same rate as non-Catholics. You contracept at the same rate. You sodomize at the same rate. You even divorce and abort at the same rate. So where the rubber meets the road, what's the answer to the question: What difference does it make to be a Catholic in America today?"

I shook my head, not knowing.

"That's the answer", he said: "None. None. Absolutely none at all."

"But should we expect to be so much better than everyone else?"

"Of course!" he answered, surprised. "What good is religion if it doesn't make you better?"

"But all religions make you better, don't they? So, if that's where the rubber meets the road, all religions are equal, aren't they?"

Exasperated, like a teacher with a hopeless student, he almost threw down his stone tablets in despair. He started to point to them to make his point, then changed his strategy. He screwed up his patience and tried again. "Look, you're a Catholic, am I right?"

"Right."

"Why?"

"Why? In twenty-five words or less? I wrote a bunch of books—"

"No, no", he wailed. "One word is enough."

"What word?"

"Try *truth*, okay? You're a Catholic because you believe what the Church says is true, right? Is there any other honest reason for believing anything?"

"Of course not."

"Okay, now what does the Church claim to be true about herself?"

"That she is the Body of Christ, both visible and invisible."

"Oooh, good for you! Sounds like you remember a little catechism, yes? Well, if that's what she is, how could she be equal to anything else? How could all religions be equal if only one of them is the visible and invisible Body of God incarnate? How could the body of men be equal to the Body of Christ? How could all churches be equal if only one of them is the one He gave as His sign to the world?"

"But isn't it arrogant to say that?" I objected.

"Arrogant? Arrogant is when you edit God's mail instead of delivering it. Hey, believe me, I know. I got a lot of God's mail in my day, and for one little editing job at Meribah I got sacked from the Promised Land trip. Let me tell you what arrogance is. Arrogance is singing Sinatra's song, 'I Did It My Way'. He gives you a Law, you take it. He gives you a Bible, you take it. He gives you a Church, you take it. Don't change a jot or a tittle. Especially a tittle. You get in all kinds of trouble changing tittles."

"Are you telling me the Church is totally right and everybody else is wrong? Are you telling me Buddhists and Muslims and Confucians aren't saved?"

"What, are you deaf? Did I say that?"

"No. So then are Buddhism and Islam and Confucianism also ways of salvation?"

"I didn't say that either. No, there's only one way. He *said*

He was the only way—were you listening? If He's wrong about that, He's not a true way at all, and He's not only wrong, but He's arrogant. (And totally meshugge to boot!) But if He's right, well, then, He's right, and those other people are not other saviors. So whether He's right or whether He's wrong, in either case He's not equal to them. He's less if He's wrong; He's more if He's right. Didn't you ever take a course in logic?"

"So Christianity is the only way to be saved?"

"*Christ* is the only way: '*the* way, and *the* truth, and *the* life'. That's a useful little word, *the*."

"So all non-Christians are wrong? Is that what you're say-ing?"

"Where they contradict the Church, of course! Or did some mafioso rub out the Law of Non-Contradiction last year? Did I miss that on the news, maybe?"

My mind couldn't resist his argument, but my prejudices could. "That all sounds very logical, Moses, but . . ."

"Is that bad? To be logical? You want instead illogical? A little muddleheaded, maybe? What, you think God is a pop psychologist? You know, sometimes I think your religion is to be nice, to be accepted, to be just like everybody else. I thought it had something to do with following a man on a cross . . ."

I suddenly realized my double folly. First, as Confucius had said, I wanted to be accepted, to be popular, rather than to be a prophet. But, even more crucially, I had planned in all four parts of this chapter to say something abstract, and this was corrected by my four teachers to something concrete. I had planned something ideological, and I was corrected to some-thing real: the Man on the Cross. I pulled out my Rosary again and looked at its crucifix. And as I looked at it, every-thing else faded away in its light: Moses and Muhammad and Buddha and Confucius and the wave that had swamped me and brought me there and the Heavenly beach—it all faded away. And, like an earlier Peter coming down from the Mount of Transfiguration, I saw "Jesus only".

And that was enough.

Chapter Seven

Is There Such a Thing as "Mere Christianity"?

A Trialogue with C. S. Lewis, Martin Luther, and Thomas Aquinas

Preface

What am I, a philosopher, doing out of my field writing on Luther and Aquinas, who were theologians, and Lewis, who was a literary critic?

A philosopher is never out of his field. His field is Everything. A philosopher will philosophize about his soup.

For another thing, Lewis intended to be a philosopher. But when no position was open in philosophy at Oxford, he took one in English literature. Lewis was also an amateur theologian—the best kind, the kind the apostles were.

Luther, Aquinas, and Lewis were all Christians, theologians, and philosophers. So am I.

What follows is a trialogue, in the double sense of "a conversation among three people", and a "trial dialogue", an exploration. The three points I want to explore in my trialogue are:

First, that Luther and Aquinas do not teach different religions but different theologies.

Second, that these theological differences are rooted in philosophical differences. And that to a large extent, therefore, the differences between Lutheranism and Catholicism are rooted in philosophical differences. And for that reason philosophy is needed to explore them and perhaps to help resolve them.

The third point is the most important one: Is there such a thing as "mere Christianity"? Is that a mere abstract "lowest common denominator"? Is it a religion distinct from Catholicism and Protestantism? What else?

The scene: C. S. Lewis is sitting alone late at night at his big oak desk at The Kilns, Oxford, writing *Mere Christianity*, his little masterpiece that is destined to enlighten millions of minds and help convert hundreds of souls. He has written everything except the introduction. (Good authors usually delay their introductions for the same reason good matchmakers do: they first have to get to know what they are to introduce.)

Lewis suddenly sits up with a start. He seems to see two visitors sitting in his room. He rubs his eyes, but the two visitors do not disappear. One is a very large, very fat Dominican friar, white-robed and tonsured. He is apparently in a fit of absent-minded abstraction. The other is a black-robed Augustinian monk, only a little less formidably fat.

As one trained in philosophy, Lewis first thinks there are four possibilities: These two creatures must come from either Heaven, Hell, Purgatory, or Central Casting. Then he thinks a fifth possibility more likely: from his own imagination. He will never settle this question in his mind with certainty, though he will enjoy an hour's conversation with them that is so lively it makes the fifth possibility unlikely.

The two visitors speak in English, but with accents. Lewis can't help associating the Dominican's accent with the Mafia and the Augustinian's with the Gestapo. By an effort of will and charity, he exorcises these thoughts, and he is rewarded by divine providence in that the two figures do not disappear but continue speaking.

LUTHER: What are you writing there, Brother Jack?

LEWIS: Are you . . . Brother Martin?

LUTHER: That habit you have of answering a question with another question—are you a rabbi or a psychiatrist?

LEWIS (*laughing*): Neither. Only a writer. I'm just finishing up preparing some talks I gave on the BBC for publication. Or I think I am, anyway. Seeing the two of you, I'm not so sure what's real any more.

AQUINAS: We are real, I assure you. And we are really privileged to meet you. For you labor at the same honorable task as we did.

LUTHER: We are here to help you finish your book: the title and the introduction. And to reassure you that this little book will be a mighty weapon in the Spirit's hands.

LEWIS: I am honored. And intrigued. May I ask you some questions?

LUTHER: No.

LEWIS (*surprised at his brusqueness*): "No?"

AQUINAS: We are here to ask *you* some questions.

LUTHER: About this book of yours. Especially the title. You are thinking of borrowing Baxter's phrase "mere Christianity". Now, what do you mean by that?

LEWIS: If you know so much of my mind, you must know the answer to that.

AQUINAS: We only know what God lets us know of your

mind. But even if we knew all that is in your mind, *you* do not. (Not yet.) We are sent to question you so that you may know it better, just as God sent his angel to Job with questions, not answers, for the same reason: God is Socratic.

LUTHER: To speak plainly, is this "mere Christianity" of yours some kind of alternative to Protestantism or Catholicism? Is it a way for someone to avoid that choice? Is it that for you? Is it a comfortable Anglicanism? A *via media*?

AQUINAS: We know, Brother Jack, that Roman Catholicism was the one subject you would not discuss, even with your friends. Why?

LEWIS: So many hard questions! I must be as candid as I can with you, I think. Brothers, as God knows, the main reason I had—or the main reason I honestly thought I had—for not discussing this rift between the churches was shame. I am ashamed of this rift as of a dirty family scandal. It is a public wound in the Body of Christ, and an ugly one, not a sanctified and glorious one like the wounds of the martyrs or the wound "Doubting Thomas" was invited to touch. I pray daily for its healing.

Also, I did not speak or write of this publicly because I thought our Lord did not want me to. I think He deliberately placed me here at the "mere" center of the battle line where the need for defense is the greatest but the defenders are few. He may have sent others on advanced theological sorties to conquer new territories, but He sent me to defend the fundamentals. That is why I broadcast these radio talks and wrote this book.

AQUINAS: Your motives are honest and holy. But do you not perhaps also fear to face the choice and to face the uncompromising claims of the Church in an uncompromising way, as you *did* face the uncompromising claims of Christ? You defended well the old argument about Him: "either God or a bad man", but not merely a good man. What about the parallel argument about the claims of the Catholic Church? She claims uniqueness and infallibility, as no other church does. She is either right or wrong in this. If she is right, she is very right, and it is your duty to bow to her, enter her, and serve her as Christ's visible body on earth.

LUTHER: And if she is wrong, she is very wrong, intolerably arrogant, even blasphemous; and it is your duty to expose her and oppose her with all your heart for the same reason: out of love for the Lord.

LEWIS: I do not know how to answer this question.

AQUINAS: By remaining outside the Catholic Church, you have already answered it.

LEWIS: My reason is moved by the Catholic arguments but also by some of the anti-Catholic arguments. But my feelings and instincts are those of a son of Ulster. But surely you two now know. Surely you can tell me the whole truth. Which of you was wrong? Surely you are not reluctant to admit your errors now.

LUTHER: We are not permitted to tell you these things, Brother Jack.

AQUINAS: We were sent to teach you, not to tell you. Perhaps we can help you find the truth for yourself.

LEWIS: I am grateful for any help you will give me. How?

LUTHER: We will argue for our respective creeds as we did on earth, without correcting any of our errors. If Brother Thomas is now a Protestant, or even a Lutheran, he will conceal it; and if I am a Roman Catholic now, or even a Thomist, I will conceal that. Now gird the loins of your mind, Brother Jack.

LEWIS: One question before you begin, if you please.

LUTHER: Ask.

LEWIS: If all you will tell me is what you said on earth, which I already know, how do I even know you are not my own unconscious?

LUTHER: That also you shall not know.

LEWIS (*sighing*): I accept my ignorance if it is God's will.

AQUINAS: That is why we were sent to you. God does not send great graces to the greedy.

LEWIS: Even if the greed is for truth? Surely we cannot be too passionate in thirsting for the truth?

AQUINAS: That depends.

LEWIS: On what?

AQUINAS: Let me test you. Do you think that finding the truth is the very first thing to care about?

LEWIS: Certainly.

AQUINAS: That is what I feared: you are too greedy, if we are to follow the example of Brother Socrates.

Lewis: What? I am amazed to hear you say that, especially invoking the name of Socrates. What could come before finding the truth?

AQUINAS: Have you considered seeking it first?

LEWIS (*smiling*): *Touché*. I am duly confounded.

AQUINAS: And so our task is not to feed you but to make you hungry.

LEWIS: But in the name of truth itself, Brothers, I declare to you that my desire to know the truth about the claims of the churches is no idle curiosity. My heart beats wildly to know this truth so that my hand and my pen can serve it. Will God not honor that motive?

AQUINAS: He will. But in His time and in His way.

LUTHER: You see, in His providence, He knows that you could not fulfill His battle plan for you as well if you knew these things. You could not have written this book, for one thing. It would have been a different book, written only to half of Christendom.

LEWIS: I see. And I accept.

LUTHER: Then accept also the task of answering our questions. Tell me, is this "mere Christianity" of yours an alternative creed to Augsburg or Trent?

LEWIS: No. It is the Apostles' Creed, the foundation of both. My hope is that returning to the common foundation may help heal the hurt and solve the split.

AQUINAS: Good. But then how is "mere Christianity" related to the churches?

LEWIS: As a hallway is related to the rooms that open off it. A hallway is not to live in. All the food and fire, bed and board, are in the rooms. The hallway is an entering place, not a stopping place.

LUTHER: Good. Put that thought into your book. Make that clear in your introduction, so that you do not further split the Church by helping to found another denomination, "mereism". For otherwise, your readers will be tempted to deal with their doubts by remaining in the hall.

LEWIS: Oh, I don't think many people would be that foolish.

LUTHER: You are mistaken. There will be a great temptation to do just that. It will even be a kind of good temptation.

LEWIS: I don't understand.

LUTHER: I am allowed to tell you this much of the future. Soon, Christians will desperately need to stand together against a common enemy. This need will be so great that there will be a temptation to "mere-ism". When the devil knocks at your door, there is no time for family squabbles.

LEWIS: Why will the need be so great? How will the devil knock at the door?

LUTHER: Before your century is over, the world will sink so spectacularly into decadence that blasphemy and pornography the likes of which you have not imagined will be protected by law and the most innocent and inoffensive public pieties will be forbidden, such as prayer in public schools. The Ten Commandments will be torn down from all public places, and in their place will be put homoerotic and sado-masochistic art more blatant than your darkest youth conceived. The law will forbid the display of Christ in a Christmas crèche but will protect the display of Christ in a jar of an artist's urine—I cannot even speak the blasphemous title of this abomination of desolation. Millions of mothers will be persuaded to slaughter their unborn sons and daughters every year. One-third of all babies conceived will be aborted. The law will remove all protection from these holy innocents, and the media will cooperate by lies, censorship, and brainwashing—a brainwash in blood. The most dreaded sexually transmitted disease will be children. Half of all marriages will fail. In the large cities, most children will be illegitimate. Parents will lose control of their children in slow, insidious increments. Virginity will become a stigma and a rarity, fornication a norm. Public schools will confiscate Bibles and distribute condoms. Propaganda for masturbation, fornication, contraception, abortion, and sodomy will be disguised as "sex education" and forced upon little children . . .

LEWIS (*eyes getting wider at each detail*): This is incredible, even to a Puddleglum like me. Do you mean these awful things will happen in Russia and her satellites?

LUTHER: No. They will not happen there. A century of prayers for Russia will be answered. The demon Communism will die in the Kremlin and migrate to American universities. Russian public schools will beg for Bibles even as American schools forbid them.

LEWIS: This is incredible—far beyond my wildest fears. Why do you tell me this?

LUTHER: So that you may understand why your book will help. Christians of all churches will be forged together by fire like the broken shards of a sword. Catholics and Protestants will be thrown in jail together by the thousands for protesting the holocaust of babies to Moloch. Thus the "good temptation" I spoke of, the temptation to abandon the rooms for the hall. Make sure you alert them to that danger.

LEWIS: Thank you, Brother Martin. I will.

AQUINAS: I have another question about "mere Christianity", Brother Jack. If it is the Apostles' Creed, as you say, is it merely twelve propositions? Is it abstracted from the fuller creeds of all the churches as a kind of creedal Lowest Common Denominator? Is it a universal abstracted from its particulars? In that case it would be a theological hall instead of a room. On the other hand, if it is concrete rather than abstract, would that not make it a third church, a rival room to the Catholic one and the Protestant ones?

LEWIS: That is a terrible dilemma, but I think I can escape between the horns. It is neither; it is the Gospel. That is concrete, not abstract: something solid and substantial. What Protestants and Catholics share is concrete. It is Christ Himself and faith in Him. Surely, whether Christ is divine is more important than whether the Pope is infallible. Surely, whether Christ is our Lord is more important than whether Mary is our Lady.

AQUINAS: Yes, but to say that one thing is greater than another is not to say that the other is not great. Angels are greater than men; love is greater than knowledge; and Christ is greater than His saints. Yet these second things are all very great.

LEWIS: True, Brother Thomas. But I must know just *how* great or important the distinctively Catholic doctrines are. All the Catholic doctrines that Brother Martin rejected because he could not find them clearly in Scripture—are these essentials or accidentals? If they are accidental, then "mere Christianity" is the only essential and amounts to Protestantism. If they are essentials, then "mere Christianity" is a mere abstraction.

AQUINAS: And now *I* escape from the horns of *your* dilemma. There are three possibilities, not two: the essence, a mere accident, or an essential property, or proper accident. Our Lord's divinity and Resurrection are essential. If one denies them, he is simply not a Christian. Latin in the liturgy and fasting on Friday are changeable accidents. But the authority of the one visible Church and our Lord's Real Presence in the Eucharist are not accidents but properties of the essence. They flow from the essence, though they are not the essence. So the dispute is neither about the essence nor the accidents but about the properties.

No Christian would disagree with Augustine's great formula, "In essentials, unity; in nonessentials, diversity; in all things, charity." But we disputed among ourselves about the *properties* of the "essentials". That is why we did not have unity. If we had disputed only about accidents, we would not have formed different denominations around them; if we had disputed about the essence, we would not both be Christians and would not be *seeking* unity. We served the same Christ but different visible churches and sacraments. We believed the same Savior but different theologies of salvation.

Would you agree with that, Brother Martin?

LUTHER: Yes, and I say the same about *sola scriptura* and *sola fide* and *sola gratia* as you say about the Church. These are essential properties.

LEWIS: That makes the notion "mere Christianity" problematic then. For a Catholic would not say that Catholicism is "mere Christianity" *plus* the Church; and a Lutheran would not say that Lutheranism is "mere Christianity" *plus* justification by faith. For these are not accidents but essential properties, and one of you, it seems, must be in error about these essential properties—as if one should say that a man's laugh was the same as a hyena's, or that speech had no meaning beyond itself, as if one de-constructed speech itself (to coin a barbarism). These are mistakes about essential properties, and very serious mistakes indeed.

LUTHER: Beware coining barbarisms, Brother Jack. Your satiric coinage may become the coin of the realm for another's philosophy some day.

AQUINAS: Your "mere Christianity" cannot be another "Christianity-plus" or a "Christianity-minus". You must neither add nor subtract, lest you create "another gospel", a *new* Christianity, which would be the opposite of *mere* Christianity.

LEWIS: But, Brothers, one of you must have done just that. Either Brother Martin subtracted Catholicism from Christianity or the Catholic Church added to it. The dispute, therefore, is about what "mere Christianity" *is*. So to avoid this dispute in my book, I must take an agreed-upon set of propositions—essentially the Apostles' Creed—as a lowest common denominator, it seems.

AQUINAS: But that is an abstraction. As I have written, the primary object of faith is not propositions, but Christ. Propositions define the faith, but they are not its primary object.

LUTHER: So make sure your book is centered on Christ. The purpose of each syllable you write must be the same as the purpose of each stone in each church building and each penny in each collection plate: to save lost souls for Christ.

AQUINAS: And to sanctify them.

LUTHER: And not to turn them to disputes about the relationship between justification and sanctification, nor to Catholic Christianity or to Lutheran Christianity or to "mere Christianity" as an abstraction, but to the concrete person of Christ.

LEWIS: Indeed I shall endeavor to be ubiquitously christocentric. But do you say creeds count but little?

LUTHER: Surely not. But the creed is for the deed.

LEWIS: What a strange thing for *you* to say! Do you mean faith is for works?

LUTHER: No, I mean that you must turn your readers' minds

to Christ so that they will turn their hearts to Him. I speak of the deed of faith.

AQUINAS: Is your purpose clear now, Brother Jack?

LEWIS: It is. Thank you. But I can't let myself miss this opportunity to try to clarify those properties you disputed. You two clearly have the same *religion* but different *theologies*. If you will not tell me directly what is true and what is false theologically, will you teach me in some other way?

LUTHER: We will. That is part of our task here. And for that, we will argue as we did on earth, and you shall be the judge.

AQUINAS: We will have something like a Scholastic Disputation, a short, formal, and logical debate.

LEWIS: Often I have dreamed of traveling back in time to hear you or Abelard or Erasmus or Cajetan! And now time has traveled forward to me. I look forward to the entertainment of a lifetime.

LUTHER: We are not sent for entertainment but for instruction.

LEWIS: Of course. But as the saying goes, "Before you shoot the arrow of truth, dip it in honey." I thank you for the honey as well as for the arrow.

AQUINAS: Let the play begin. We will play ourselves, as we were. You will be the judge. Brother Martin, as the protester, will begin. We will be controversial but friendly, even playful, as we play old parts, now totally free from the old rancorous and divisive feelings of hate and fear. We will engage in polemics but in a nonpolemical way, as playing a part—a serious part, but one we can distinguish ourselves from, as polemicists of the past could not. They put themselves on the stage; we put ourselves in the audience, watching ourselves act these parts.

LUTHER: I begin, then, by questioning the very notion of a "mere Christianity" common to both churches. Granted, Christ is common to both of us, for we come from Heaven, not from Hell. But there is no common foundation to our two churches. You must say that the Protestant churches are heretical or schismatic; and I say the Roman Catholic Church is apostate, for it preaches a different Scripture, a different salvation, and a different sovereignty. A different Scripture because it has added the traditions of men to the Word of God. A different salvation because it replaces the gospel of salvation by faith with the Galatian gospel of salvation by works. And a different sovereignty, the sovereignty of man's so-called free will rather than the sovereignty of God and His grace.

My three formulas are shields against these three deadly darts of error: *sola scriptura* against the claim of the Church to add a second scripture; *sola fide* against the claims of good works to add a second salvation; and *sola gratia* against the claims of the human will to add a second sovereignty to the sovereignty of God.

First, *sola scriptura*. All our differences begin here, in the epistemology. The reason I reject all the Catholic doctrines I reject is that I do not find them in Scripture. *Sola scriptura* is my skeleton key. Whatever doctrinal doors this key opens, I will enter; whatever doors this key does not open, I will not enter. Now, Brother Jack, if you too confine yourself to the teachings found in Scripture in your book, then "mere Christianity" is simply another word for Protestantism.

Second, *sola fide*. The Catholic Church preaches a different gospel. For Romans and Galatians clearly teach that a man is justified by faith alone, without the works of the law. And this law is the moral law, not simply the liturgical law, as some of your contemporary Catholic apologists have claimed. Here you not only add to Scripture, you contradict it—and on the single most important question in the world: What must I do to be saved? Catholics simply do not know how to get to Heaven! They have a wrong road map. If some of them get to Heaven, as you did, Brother Thomas, it is not because of their maps but in spite of them.

Third, *sola gratia*. Catholic theology is half-Christian and half-pagan, or humanist; for it gives to man the role of allowing or not allowing God's grace to work—the role of freely cooperating in his own salvation. The sale of indulgences was only one spectacular example of this deeper principle. The principle is that of paganism: dealing with the deity. It is the pagan gods we can make contracts with; the God of Abraham, Isaac, and Jacob is sovereign. It is pagan man who proudly thinks of his own will as sovereign and free; Christian man knows his will is in bondage; for he is a sinner, and every sinner is a *slave* of sin and can be saved only by God's grace.

Now, what "mere Christianity" is left common to these clear and liberating principles of *sola scriptura*, *sola fide*, and *sola gratia*, on the one hand, and the Catholic compromises and corruptions of them, on the other hand?

It is your turn now, Brother Thomas, to obfuscate my simple scriptural statements with your Scholastic subtleties and sophistries.

AQUINAS: I shall try to answer all your arguments as clearly and directly as you put them, and in an equally short time.

LUTHER: If I were a betting man, I would bet half my fortune that you will not do it. You will not even meet my time. You are slow and fat, and I run much faster than you do. You Italians never took time seriously. Only one man ever made your trains run on time—Mussolini—and that was hailed as a miracle that proved he was the Messiah.

AQUINAS: And were it not for this Italian ineptitude with clocks, your fellow-countryman, a certain Adolf Hitler, would not have had Mussolini as his ally, would not have had to delay his Russian campaign until he had rescued Mussolini's farcically failed invasion of Yugoslavia, and would have won Moscow, Stalingrad, and Leningrad, thus Russia, thus the war, and thus the world. So the world was saved by Italian ineptitude with time!

LUTHER: What is the point of this new theory of history, Brother Thomas?

AQUINAS: The point is simply that I can condense my arguments much more than you can, Brother Martin.

LUTHER: Really? How many pages did your little "Summary of Theology" run to? You said in the introduction that it was for "beginners". About six thousand pages, wasn't it? And you didn't even finish it!

AQUINAS: I couldn't. In light of what I saw, all I said was only straw.

LUTHER: Well, you got that right, anyway.

AQUINAS: Wasn't that exactly what you called the Epistle of James? I would rather call my own words straw than another's, and certainly rather call man's words straw than God's!

(*As Luther is about to pick up an inkwell to throw at Aquinas— playfully, for, after all, they come from Heaven, where play was invented—Lewis interrupts.*)

LEWIS: Brothers, is this sort of Scholastic Disputation practiced in the University of Heaven? Please fight only with an inkwell shaped into words.

LUTHER: Aha! Brother Jack is a punster after my own heart—so unlike your heavy-handed literalism, Brother Thomas.

AQUINAS: Literalism? Have you never heard of my doctrine of analogy? Even the word "being" is a pun in my philosophy.

LEWIS: I am amused but not instructed, gentlemen. Brother Thomas, are you stalling for time, or can you answer Brother Martin's three charges?

AQUINAS: I am happy to answer.

First, most of our theological differences are indeed rooted in the epistemology of *sola scriptura*. I do not say *all* of them, for some are rooted in our metaphysics. Your Nominalism is the root of your "federal" theory of justification, for instance.

I deny *sola scriptura* because it is self-contradictory. Scripture alone does not teach "Scripture alone". *Sola scriptura* is a human theology—yours—added to Scripture.

Second, Scripture gives the label of "the pillar and ground of the truth", not to itself, but to the Church.

Third, you misunderstand Catholic claims for the Church. She is not a second, separate, rival source of truth, a second book, a second data. She teaches, interprets, protects, and defends her original data, "the deposit of faith", which is virtually identical to Scripture. She is one (and only one) living teacher with one (and only one) living book.

Fourth, the inevitable consequences in history of *sola scriptura* have been endless fissiparation and denominationalism—the very thing Scripture itself frequently warns against and our Lord prayed against in His high priestly prayer before His Passion (Jn 17). By Brother Jack's day now, there are already twenty thousand different non-Catholic denominations! Surely Saint Paul was right to be utterly aghast at even the three or four denominations he saw arising in Corinth and mercilessly to put that evil cancer to death before it could metastasize.

Sola scriptura without one authoritative Church to interpret Scripture means that each pupil interprets the teacher's textbook in his own way, not the teacher's way, thus rendering the teacher superfluous. Eventually, there will be as many interpretations as pupils, in effect as many textbooks as pupils. Thus *sola scriptura* undermines the authority of the very Scripture it exalts. The logical conclusion of private interpretation is private churches—eventually as many Protestantisms as Protestants.

Fifth, there is the causal argument. A fallible cause cannot produce an infallible effect. But the Church is the efficient cause of Scripture. She wrote it. She is also its formal cause: she defined its canon. Thus, if the Church is only fallible, her canon of Scripture is only fallible, and we do not know infallibly which books *are* Scripture, that is, infallible. So again your *sola scriptura* doctrine demeans the authority of the very Scripture you want to exalt.

Sixth, the undermining of scriptural authority by skeptical, naturalistic, and modernist hermeneutics has in fact plunged half of Protestant denominations into this heretical chaos. Though many individual Catholic Scripture scholars are also Modernists, the Church has never been and never will be. So again, your denial of Church authority has undermined scriptural authority.

On your second major point, *sola fide*, I wonder whether our apparent contradiction about justification by faith masks a real agreement. For I agree that faith alone can justify, as Saint Paul clearly says; and I think you agree that good works are the inevitable fruit of real, saving faith. You further agree that *intellectual* faith alone does not justify (for "the devils also believe, and tremble") *and* that the greatest of the three "theological virtues" of faith, hope, and charity is not faith but charity, as this same Apostle says. And I agree that man cannot buy his way into Heaven with good works (for "all our righteousness is as filthy rags"). And you do not say that it doesn't matter what we do once we believe. Do you see, Brother?—how we are misunderstood and caricatured by each other's apologists?

I also agree that the fruits of faith are often missing among Catholics. But they are also often missing among Protestants. Does this disprove Protestant theology? A man named Chesterton, who wrote the best book there is about me, said that the one great argument against Christianity is Christians.

But doctrinal truth cannot be proved by taking the spiritual temperature of its adherents. Heretics can be very moral and very sincere, and truth-speaking authorities can be wicked. The Borgia popes were libertines, murderers, and hypocrites, yet they sat in Peter's chair. The Pharisees sat in Moses' seat, and therefore our Lord commanded his disciples to obey them, though He cautioned them not to imitate their works.

By the way, no one of those wicked popes ever changed the Church's teachings, even when he scorned them. Why would a man not shatter the mirror that shows his faults, unless this mirror is divinely protected? So I use the very data you bring against the Church—her corruption—to prove her providential and miraculous protection and survival.

Finally, *sola gratia*. I agree with *sola gratia*, and so does the Council of Trent. But like Augustine (whom you also claim as your teacher), I also believe in free will. For like Augustine, I embrace both sides of the paradox at the heart of all the mysteries of the faith, from the Trinity through the Incarnation to the physical-yet-spiritual nature of man.

Augustine says all men have free *will* (*liberum arbitrium*) by nature, but only the redeemed have *liberty*, or freedom from sin (*libertas*), by grace. You deny free will because you see it as a doctrine of pagan humanism. But it is not. Free will is part of God's image in us. And it is wholly dependent on grace, both for being created and for being redeemed. Our very free cooperation with grace is also an effect of grace, as I said in my "little" *Summa*, if you had only read it.

I do not hold that half our salvation comes from us and half from God. It all comes from God. It is like the relationship between an author and his characters. Odysseus' choices are free, and are his, and also they are predestined and are Homer's. For God, our sovereign Author, decrees us to be free. God is your Homer. He is your Father, not your godfather; he does not make you an offer you can't refuse.

LUTHER: Are you finished playing with your straw, Brother Thomas?

AQUINAS: I am.

LUTHER: Well, then, let us tie things up. We promised to examine Brother Jack's concept of "mere Christianity". But we seem to differ so radically about what Christianity *is* that the very notion of some common essence seems now in jeopardy.

AQUINAS: Not so, Brother Martin.

LUTHER: How so, Brother Thomas, if you deny and I affirm all three of my *sola*s?

AQUINAS: I affirm them all, too, in their proper sense. But we need the care and patience of a philosopher to define their proper sense.

LUTHER: Then kindly explain, Master Philosopher, to this plain peasant how you can affirm *sola scriptura* when you believe in all the extrascriptural dogmas of the Church too?

AQUINAS: The formula *sola scriptura* is correct materially but not formally. The raw material, the content, the data of faith are all in Scripture. But the Church defines it, formalizes it, in her creeds.

LUTHER: If the data for all Catholic teachings have to be in Scripture, then you had better abandon your Marian dogmas, for they are not there.

AQUINAS: Their data is. *She* is.

LUTHER: But Scripture is nearly silent about her. A few scant verses. You have erected an enormous building on a tiny foundation that cannot bear its weight.

AQUINAS: Can an acorn bear the weight of an oak tree?

LUTHER: You cannot argue from analogy, especially not a natural and material analogy.

AQUINAS: Then I will argue from a theological one, if you permit me. The immense edifice of trinitarian dogma as defined by the ecumenical councils of the first six centuries, which you hold as well as I, also rests on a relatively small textual foundation in Scripture. And a mysterious one—look how easily many heretics misunderstood the data in many different ways. The metaphor of the tree is apt: the dogmas of the Church grow gradually from within, as a tree grows, not as a building grows, from without. So my biological analogy is more apt than your technological one.

LUTHER: Then let me try a third image. The Catholic has two horses pulling his chariot—Church and Scripture—while the Protestant has only one. Surely it cannot be both—two and only one. Surely there is a simple contradiction here between us.

AQUINAS: There is only one horse, but it needs one rider. There is only one divine book, but it needs one divine interpreter.

LUTHER: Your analogy is again not apt—

AQUINAS: The horses were your analogy, Brother Martin, not mine.

LUTHER: You supplied the rider, Brother; I supplied only the horse.

AQUINAS: You may win the metaphor, Brother Martin. But you have not yet won the point.

LUTHER: The point is that the metaphor is wrong. The rider is the master of his horse, but the Church is not the master of Scripture but its servant.

AQUINAS: I agree! As the interpreter is the servant of his textbook.

LUTHER: But anyone can see that *this* interpreter is no longer the humble servant of his textbook but the author of a second textbook. It is not a thing that is difficult to see. It is empirical. Anyone can compare the dogmas of the Church with Scripture and see that the Church is adding, not just interpreting. Half of your dogmas are nowhere in Scripture at all, and half again of those flatly contradict Scripture. For instance—

LEWIS: Excuse me for interrupting, gentlemen, but I fear you are now about to open a Pandora's box, a can of worms —worms without end, amen. Could you please focus on the issue of Church and Scripture by itself instead of voyaging off into strange new seas? I think I have not got all the time in the world.

AQUINAS: Exactly what I was going to suggest. We Scholastics cultivated that habit of arguing about only one thing at a time.

LUTHER: Fine. I will make my point about the Church with still another image, then. What I did was to *reform* the Church, not refound it. It was like scraping barnacles off a ship, off the Ark of the Church. I restored it to its God-designed form, which had become *de*formed by being encrusted with the barnacles of human additions.

AQUINAS: So you believe—to put the point as simply and baldly as possible—that our Lord created a Protestant Church and we Catholicized her, or Romanized her, while *we* believe that our Lord created a Catholic church and you Protestantized her, you trimmed the Ark down to a sailboat.

LUTHER: Plainly put, that is our essential difference about Church history.

AQUINAS: Good. Then the issue is empirically testable. Historical research will show one position or the other. And I claim it will show the continuity of Catholic dogma and the roots of that dogma in the earliest writings of the Church Fathers. Many a Catholic convert has trod this path to Rome, the historical path—for instance, Cardinal Newman. All the distinctively Catholic doctrines are to be found there very early in Church history, though some more clearly than others. And *none* of the distinctively Protestant denials of Catholic doctrines is there, except in those writers who were identified by the universal Church as heretics.

LUTHER: So you claim. But I claim the same for Scripture as you claim for the Church Fathers: that an empirical, factual investigation will reveal that the Church Christ founded was Protestant, not Catholic. You claim to prove Catholicism by finding it in the Fathers; I claim to prove Protestantism by finding it in Scripture. And just as you claim not to find any distinctively Protestant doctrines in the Fathers, I claim not to find any distinctively Catholic doctrines in Scripture.

AQUINAS: Then we must compare Catholic doctrine with
Scripture, and Protestant doctrine with the Fathers, and see
which claim is proved wrong by the facts. And remember, the
argument from silence proves nothing. You must prove that
Scripture *contradicts* Catholic doctrine, and I must prove that
from the beginning the teaching of the Church, as shown in
the writings of the Fathers, *contradicts* Protestant doctrine.
Now, how do you propose we begin this investigation?

LUTHER: Brother Thomas, you must be in one of your famous fits of absent-mindedness again. We do not have the
time for such an investigation here, for we are on earth, not in
Heaven, and we are here for Brother Jack, who is under time
constraints. He is mortal, unlike us. He lacks unlimited lei-
sure.

AQUINAS: How unfortunate!

LUTHER: I suggest we confine our argument to Scripture.

AQUINAS: Such a procedure assumes *sola scriptura* at least in
practice. But that is the very question under dispute. So you
seem to beg the question.

LUTHER: No. I want to move to the second *sola*—*sola fide*,
the most crucial one because it is about what I must do to be
saved. And since we both accept the authority of Scripture, I
can argue from it that Romans and Galatians clearly teach *sola
fide*, whether *sola scriptura* is true or not.

AQUINAS: But I accept *sola fide* too in the proper sense, just as
I accept *sola scriptura* in the proper sense, as I said before. I
accept *sola gratia* too, since that too is in Scripture.

LUTHER: But you do *not* accept these three principles. Your
"proper sense" is an *im*proper sense. You do not accept them
as they are meant.

AQUINAS: Not as *you* mean them, no. But as Scripture and Church mean them, yes. You are not my authority, after all; Scripture and Church are.

LUTHER: You do *not* accept them as Scripture teaches them. You contradict Scripture.

AQUINAS: You think I do. And I think you do. Neither of us can be the judge of the both of us. You see? That is why we need the authority of the Church to decide between us.

LUTHER: No, we need the authority of Scripture to decide between us.

AQUINAS: But we both accept the authority of Scripture, and yet we disagree. Therefore that authority alone—Scripture alone—cannot in fact resolve disagreements. What we see happening here is the history of the Church in miniature. And in this little laboratory we see how private interpretation alone inevitably leads to error.

LUTHER: It does not. The Spirit will keep us one and keep us from error if only we submit to His leading. The Spirit, not the Pope. Do you not think the instruments in God's orchestra would play in harmony if only they followed the Conductor's baton?

AQUINAS: True. But I think I can prove to you that private interpretation leads to error, if you let me ask you a few questions in the Socratic style.

LUTHER: Ask away. I do not fear your Catholicized Socrates.

AQUINAS: Do you think my Catholicism is from God or from me? Is it the Holy Spirit that leads me to submit to the Catholic Church and to the Pope and to believe all those teachings you reject, or is it my private human spirit?

LUTHER: Your spirit, of course.

AQUINAS: So I have fallen into error this way, you say.

LUTHER: Indeed you have.

AQUINAS: Then private interpretation leads to error.

LUTHER: This is sophistry!

AQUINAS: No, it is logic. One of two contradictories must be false. Do you dispute that?

LUTHER: No . . .

AQUINAS: And our two positions are contradictory, you say?

LUTHER: Yes. Wait—suppose I say no?

AQUINAS: Then I welcome you with open arms to union and reconciliation with Rome!

LUTHER: And if I say we *are* contradictory?

AQUINAS: Then one of the two of us has been led into error.

LUTHER: That is so.

AQUINAS: Then private interpretation has led into error.

LUTHER: No, *Roman* interpretation has led into error. *My* private interpretation, guided by Scripture and the Spirit, unlike yours, has led me into the truth.

AQUINAS: Is *all* "Roman interpretation" error? Are the Popes an infallible magisterium of error?

LUTHER: I suppose not. Not even the ACLU can be wrong all the time.

AQUINAS: And is *all* private interpretation true? Are each of the twenty thousand Protestant denominations right even where they contradict each other?

LUTHER: Of course not. But this is still sophistry, Brother Thomas. You could simply deny the clear meaning of any text in Scripture and prove from the fact that someone denies it this same pseudoconclusion, that private interpretation leads into error and that the Church must step in to interpret the Bible authoritatively. Why don't you use the same argument to prove the need for the Church to interpret Euclid? You cannot prove the need for a Church of Grammar just by committing a solecism.

AQUINAS: Euclid and grammar are clear to natural reason and generate almost no disagreements. But Scripture is full of divinely revealed mysteries and generates great disagreements.

LUTHER: Scripture is clear if only our approach is clear. The pure in heart shall see God truly. If your will is to do the will of the Father, you will understand the teaching.

AQUINAS: If Scripture is clear, why have there been so many heresies? All heretics have claimed Scripture, believed Scripture, appealed to Scripture.

LUTHER: But they have not submitted to the Spirit. The Spirit never leads astray.

AQUINAS: Indeed not, but *how can we know* which human teachers have the Spirit, and thus have the truth, and which ones only claim to have Him but do not, and thus do not have the truth—unless we have the Church to tell us publicly? Private witnesses contradict; a public witness must adjudicate.

LUTHER: The public witness is Scripture. Scripture interprets itself.

AQUINAS: What do you mean, "Scripture interprets itself"?

LUTHER: That no one who honestly seeks to know the truth from its pages will be led astray.

AQUINAS: It seems, then, that you must believe that there has never been an honest heretic.

LUTHER: And it seems *you* must believe that God gave Scripture as a puzzle for popes to unravel rather than as a light for laymen to travel by—a riddle for theologians rather than a map for all Christians.

AQUINAS: I do not believe that, any more than you believe there has never been an honest heretic. Even the best of teachers is often misunderstood when he speaks of high mysteries of the Kingdom—as was our Lord Himself misunderstood, on many occasions, by his friends as well as by his enemies.

LUTHER: So you would have the Church to improve on our Lord's teachings, eh?

AQUINAS: No; to obey His commission faithfully to explain, explore, and apply them.

LEWIS (*interrupting again*): Gentlemen, I am impressed by both your arguments, but I have heard most of them before, and I am no closer to certainty now. *I* did not mention any of these arguments in my books because I did not want to set Scripture against Church, nor Protestant against Catholic, for I have a high view of all four.

AQUINAS: A high view of both Scripture and Church sounds more Catholic than Protestant.

LUTHER: But Brother Jack included only Protestant—that is, scriptural—teachings in this book he has been writing. So "mere Christianity" is just another name for Protestant Christianity.

LEWIS: I do not agree with either of you there. "Mere Christianity" is not more Catholic than Protestant, nor is it more Protestant than Catholic. It is the common core.

LUTHER: The common core of Christianity?

LEWIS: Yes.

LUTHER: And Christianity tells us essentially about our sin and Christ's salvation, does it not?

LEWIS: Yes.

LUTHER: Then "mere Christianity" tells us what we must do to be saved?

LEWIS: Yes.

LUTHER: So if Protestants and Catholics disagree on how to be saved, there *is* no common core, no common "mere Christianity".

LEWIS: That seems to follow.

AQUINAS: It seems we have now come to the heart of our question about "mere Christianity".

LUTHER: Indeed we have, and the question before us is only the single most momentous question a man can ask in this world: "What must I do to be saved?" And the clear and simple answer of Scripture to that clear and simple question is: "Believe in the Lord Jesus Christ, and you shall be saved."

AQUINAS: And I accept that as well as you do. Do you also accept that good works are a necessary fruit of faith?

LUTHER: I do.

AQUINAS: Then we agree on two essential points.

LUTHER: But I do not agree that these good works contribute one iota to our salvation. It is faith *alone* that saves us.

AQUINAS: But you admit that the good works are at least an index of faith, like a grade in a course, do you not?

LUTHER: But the grade is not the *cause* of passing the course. It is only the effect.

AQUINAS: That is so. But it *is* a part of the whole process of education. The fruit is part of the whole process of a plant's growth, and so good works are a part of the whole process of salvation.

LUTHER: Not salvation. Not justification. Only sanctification.

AQUINAS: You admit, then, at least, that though a man can be justified by faith alone, he is not sanctified by faith alone but by works as well?

LUTHER: He is sanctified by his faith too.

AQUINAS: Is this a faith that works? Does not this faith lead to good works as surely as the seed leads to the flower, if it is truly alive?

LUTHER: That is true.

AQUINAS: So faith *works*. We both agree about that. I think we disagree about *how* it works. But that is theology. *That* it works is religion. We have the same religion, even if different theologies.

LUTHER: I am not sure I accept your analysis of our differences. Let me try to understand. How do you see our deepest differences in theology?

AQUINAS: In two places. First, the link between faith and salvation. Second, the link between faith and works. You taught a "federal theology": that the link between faith and salvation was God's legal decree. I taught that there is an ontological link, that faith and baptism actually let God's very life into our souls, as turning on a faucet lets water flow.

LUTHER: That is correct. I was a Nominalist and suspicious of such metaphysics.

AQUINAS: And the second link, between faith and good works, was for you our gratitude for being saved. But for me it is ontological again: the same supernatural life we let in by faith we let out by good works.

LUTHER: Metaphysics again!

AQUINAS: But surely the objective reality of the life and grace of God is a surer basis for a connection than the subjective feeling and response of man? *That* sounds more like humanism than Christianity!

LUTHER: That is no more humanistic than your belief that our free choice to have faith causes Christ's life to enter us. I say it is rather the reverse: the object of our faith, Christ, is the cause of our act of faith.

AQUINAS: I affirm that too. That is why I agree with your *sola gratia*. Our very free will and its choice to accept God's grace are themselves grace: created by grace and healed and inspired by grace. One of the Church's greatest saints said with her dying breath: "Everything is a grace." It is God's grace that gives us Christ. It is Christ who gives us the Spirit. It is the Spirit who gives us supernatural life in our souls. It is this life that produces our faith. Finally, this faith creates its own good works as a good tree bears good fruit. It is all one divine chain, with six golden links, laden end to end with love. Love begins it, as God's motive for grace. And the works of love end it, as the fruit of grace. When we do the works of love, that is God doing them in us through this golden chain. "God is love, and he who lives in love lives in God and God

in him"—that concrete reality is "mere Christianity".
But . . .

At this point the conversation was suddenly interrupted. All
three men were beginning to smile together as Aquinas
finished his last speech; and then two things happened simul-
taneously. First, a radio announced an apocalyptic event from
America: the Boston Red Sox had won the World Series.
Second, at this announcement the sky rolled apart like a
scroll, and all three men were raptured to Heaven. As they
ascended, they heard a Charlton Heston-like voice muttering
something about "the clearest apocalyptic sign I ever gave
them".

Perhaps we should get on with our work and complete the
dialogue they began before it's too late.

Chapter Eight

The Eucharist and Ecumenism

No Catholic dogma is so distinctive and so apparently anti-ecumenical as the dogma of the Real Presence of Christ in the Eucharist. Yet this dogma may be the greatest cause of ecumenism and eventual reunion. Here's how.

Catholics may wonder: What new can be said about the Eucharist? Perhaps the eyes of a new Catholic, a convert from Protestantism, can see the same eternal truths from a new and different angle and thus cast some new rays of light on this timeless truth

In my pilgrimage from Dutch Reformed Calvinism to Roman Catholicism, the one Catholic dogma that most drew me in was the Eucharist. Yet at the same time the Eucharist was the one Catholic dogma that loomed as my main obstacle.

Let me first try to explain its attraction. It was perhaps the single most distinctive Catholic doctrine, the most radically Catholic doctrine. It was a touchstone. If I was to become a Catholic, it would be out of love of Christ; and if Christ was really present in the Eucharist as the Church said He was, then my love for Him would have to draw me there like a magnet, away from a church where Christ was present only subjectively, in the souls of good Protestant Christians, into the Church where He was more fully present, present also objectively, in the Eucharist. As Saint Augustine says, "my love is my weight", "my love is my gravity" (*amor meus, pondus meum*). Where it goes, I go.

The doctrine of the Eucharist, however, is not self-supporting. It is not self-evident. It rests on the teaching authority of the visible Catholic Church. Why did I come to accept that teaching authority? I will tell you why.

As a Calvinist and a student at Calvin College, I became interested enough in things Catholic for these things to appear a temptation—a temptation I wanted to overcome, since it would have been very inconvenient to me, as well as painful to my family, for me to become a Catholic. So I was looking for good reasons to remain Protestant. I thought I had found one in a Church history class at Calvin College. The professor explained very clearly the difference between the Catholic and the Protestant accounts of Church history, of what essentially had happened to the Church between the time of Christ and now. He told us that some day we would meet Roman Catholics who would argue that we were in the wrong church because our church was founded only by John Calvin in the sixteenth century, while their Church was founded by Jesus Christ in the first century, and we had better have an answer ready for that argument, and the answer was as follows.

The professor picked up a piece of chalk and drew the first of two diagrams on the board. It was labeled "the Catholic account of Church history" and consisted in a line moving gradually upward, like a tree, with the trunk splitting in two in A.D. 1054, and then some branches breaking off in the sixteenth century: Luther, Calvin, Zwingli, Henry VIII. Then he drew another diagram, labeled "the Protestant account of Church history". Again the line moved onward and upward, but then it plunged gradually downward, especially after the Edict of Milan gave the Church state backing in the year 313. At the lowest point in the line's dip, in the sixteenth century, a vertical straight line arose that led back to the height reached at the beginning of the line. The professor explained the point: the Reformers had not separated themselves from the Church Christ founded; the Roman Catholic Church had done that. The Reformers had reformed and reconstituted the church, returned to it. They were not the innovators. They brought the Church back to its Christlike, New Testament form. They were not progressives, they were traditionalists. They didn't seek anything new but something old. In other words, Catholics claimed that Christ founded a Catholic Church and that the Reformers made her Protestant; but Protestants claimed that Christ founded a Protestant church and that Rome made it Catholic. Catholics claimed that the things Protestants threw out with their *sola scriptura* doctrine were present from the beginning and only grew, gradually developing from within, like a tree. Protestants claimed that the things they threw out were not in the Church that Christ founded but were foreign additions from paganism, things like barnacles, which attached themselves to the hull of the ark. The Reformers only scraped off the barnacles. The barnacles were all the distinctively Catholic doctrines that were not, according to the Protestants, clearly in Scripture, including the Mass and the Real Presence of Christ in the Eucharist.

I remember being struck by two conclusions that followed from this account. First, both Catholics and Protestants were using the same standard: Christ. Catholics fought to keep all the distinctively Catholic things *because they believed that Christ had instituted them*. And Protestants fought against these distinctively Catholic things *because they believed that Christ had* not *instituted them*. So it was the same love and loyalty to the same Christ that both united *and* divided Catholics and Protestants.

Second, I was thrilled with the thought that the whole question of Catholic versus Protestant was rationally and even empirically resolvable. It was a question of historical fact, not merely theological theory. This thought thrilled me because I wanted to prove to myself that I was in the right church, and now I had a way. I would just read the earliest Christian documents, the writings of the Church Fathers, and prove to myself how Protestant they were.

Well, any educated Catholic can write the rest of the story, especially if you've read Newman. Like him, instead of finding how Protestant the early Church was, I found how Catholic the early Church was. I became a Catholic essentially for the very concrete historical reason that I discovered that Jesus Christ had founded the Catholic Church.

There were many issues—Church unity, Church authority, Roman primacy, devotion to saints, especially Mary, prayers for the dead, Purgatory—but the most prominent issue for me in my research into early Church history was the Eucharist. I was totally bowled over by the discovery that every description of early Christian worship centered on the Eucharist and that the Real Presence was universally assumed long before it was defined. A Protestant taking a time machine back to any time at all before the Reformation would *not* feel at home. I knew that, because I was that Protestant, and history is a time machine, and I did not feel at home. He would feel that he had stumbled into a Catholic church. The center of worship was the Eucharist, not the Bible; the altar, not the pulpit; the consecration of the bread and wine, not the preaching of the sermon. Smack in the middle of the thing Christ instituted was the Eucharist, and this was no mere symbol to pre-Reformation Christians. It was Christ Himself. Even in Scripture, I found, there are passages that make no sense unless this is so, notably John 6 and 1 Corinthians 11.

So the Eucharist, above all else, brought me in by this historical route. I needed a rational route too. Rationally, the argument was this: it was an either/or argument, parallel to the famous old argument for Christ's divinity that goes *aut deus aut homo malus*, "either God or a bad man". *That* argument proves that the man who claimed to be God could not possibly be simply a good man. He must be either God or a bad man: a liar or a lunatic. Similarly, the Eucharist was either to be worshipped or to be detested as gross idolatry. If the Church was wrong here, she was horribly, blasphemously wrong, bowing to bread and worshipping wine. (But then, how could she have produced such saints?) But if she was right, she was divinely right.

I still remember the sudden shock when I realized why medieval Catholics had built the most heavenly, the most miraculous buildings ever seen on earth, Gothic cathedrals. Those miracles of stone leaping up into life and looking like angels were houses to house and glorify the Eucharist. If Catholics had not believed in Christ's Real Presence there, they could never have built those incredible buildings with such incredible passion and patience and sacrifice. Protestants did not build them, and still don't, except out of imitation of Catholics. It was the Real Presence of Christ in the Eucharist that explained the real presence of Christ in the hearts that were inspired to create those cathedrals for the Eucharist—cathedrals that make Christ present in another way, a way less real than the Eucharist and less real than the heart but still real and powerful and effective: present in stone and glass, in form and matter, as an artist is present in his art.

But—and here is the paradoxical second half of my story—this same precious doctrine of the real, objective presence of Christ in the Eucharist was the hardest thing for me to believe, my biggest obstacle in becoming a Catholic.

To explain this second half of the paradox, consider how

utterly strange and different the Catholic doctrines of the Real Presence, transubstantiation, and *ex opere operato* must appear to the Protestant mind, a mind that is utterly convinced of the Kantian principle that the only absolute good is a good will, that religion should be something spiritual (that is, interior); that Christianity is radically different from paganism in that paganism believes in idolatry and magic and ascribes spiritual efficacy to external material things and places. From this point of view, the Catholic doctrine of the Eucharist seems to a Protestant the perfect example of a regression back to paganism. It regresses from and compromises the distinctively Christian doctrine that "God is spirit, and they that worship Him must worship Him in spirit and in truth." Just as a Muslim or a Jew believes that Christianity regressed into pagan polytheism by its doctrine of the Trinity, Protestants believe Catholics regressed into pagan idolatry and became half-Christian, half-pagan with their doctrine of the Eucharist.

It's half-true: Catholicism agrees with paganism more than with Protestantism in being robustly sacramental. Catholicism is more like African religion than Scandinavian religion. Protestantism is intellectual and moral and verbal but not sacramental, except thinly and peripherally and weakly. Catholics believe pagans are right and Protestants are wrong on this issue: that God has decreed to associate spiritual power and presence with specific bits of matter (as He did with the Temple and the Ark of the Covenant) and specific times and places. The Old Testament instances of this association were foreshadowings of the Incarnation, and the Catholic Church's sacramentalism is a consequence of the Incarnation and an extension of the Incarnation. Some matter, some places, and some times are holy. Not all times are equally holy. Time is not irrelevant to holiness, or Godliness. The time of Christ was a special time, to which we return at every Mass or which we make present at every Mass. The same with place: there are holy places—churches, sanctuaries—because Christ's human body occupied one place and not another. The land He lived in was and is the "Holy Land" because He lived in it. Finally, matter, as well as time and space, is not indifferent to holiness. As the matter—the very molecules—of Christ's human body were sacred, so the material appearances of the Eucharist are sacred. The scandal of the Eucharist is nothing more than an extension of the scandal of the Incarnation.

Once you have swallowed the camel of the Incarnation, why strain at the gnat of the Eucharist? If the eternal Creator-Spirit can become a flesh-and-blood man, why can't that man's body take on the appearances of bread and wine? The gap between bread and human flesh is only finite; the gap between man and God is infinite. If God can leap the infinite gap, He can certainly leap the finite one.

But it shocked me to realize how objectively real it was. It was like surgery or travel maps. Subjective sincerity is not enough for a surgeon or a travel agent. We need objectively right things. We live in an objectively real material world, and life or death often depends on what part of matter we touch. Once God became incarnate, this became true for God too: touch the molecules of the body of John the Baptist, and you touch only a man. The hem of his garment does not heal. His blood does not redeem. But touch Christ, and you are healed. His blood makes the difference between Heaven and Hell. The Eucharist is an extension of this objective principle. Eat Protestant communion bread, and you have not eaten Christ. You have no more grace than if you had only prayed or read the Bible. But eat the Catholic Host, and you are really filled with Christ, as really as Mary's womb was.

Obviously, Christ's objectively Real Presence is better and

stronger than merely the presence of a pious subjective human intention. Obviously, if Jesus Christ in His human body were here and touched me—if I could stand at the foot of the Cross and have His blood literally spill on my tongue—I would be more graced than if I only piously *thought* about Him. But this is exactly what happens in the Eucharist. He is as really, truly, objectively, and fully present there—the very same Christ, the whole Christ, body and blood, soul and divinity—as He was present on Calvary. And the wine I drink is *not* wine but is as truly His blood as His *blood* is His blood.

A Catholic who has grown up with the Eucharist cannot, I think, appreciate the fear, the terror, and the thrill, the "too good to be true" feeling, that a Protestant naturally has when confronted with the full, authentic Catholic doctrine of the Eucharist. It really is as real as magic. No, it is more real, because magic is only like a machine, impersonal and mechanical. This is personal, like birth or lovemaking. And just as concretely real.

But we don't *feel* this tremendous thing when we receive Communion. If this is really God—more powerful than a trillion atom bombs—then why don't we *feel* touched by the power, if we *are* touched by the power?

Because Christ instituted the Eucharist partly to test and increase our faith, just as God tested Adam and Eve in Eden. The forbidden fruit didn't *look* bad. It looked good, like the other fruits. God's command seemed arbitrary and irrational. It had to be. If God had said, "Don't eat this fruit because there's a worm in it", then Adam's obedience would have been based on his own reason, not on his faith in God. God gave no reason, and no appearances, precisely so that Adam's obedience would be based on sheer faith, blind faith.

It is blind faith but not deaf faith. As Thomas Aquinas wrote in the "Adore Te Devote":

Sight, taste, and touch in Thee are each deceived;
The ear alone most safely is believed.
I believe all the Son of God has spoken:
Than Truth's own word there is no truer token.

What Adam refused in Eden, we accept in the Eucharist: to "live by faith, not by sight"; to "trust and obey, for there's no other way."

I love the Eucharist because it appeals to faith, not to feeling. Only once in my life did I ever feel anything remarkable upon receiving Communion: the very first time, my first Communion, at age twenty-one. That was a special, unusual gift, not to be repeated lest we get a spiritual sweet tooth, lest we lust for experiences and consolations, lest we lust instead of trust. The Eucharist is perfect for us because it gives us, without pain, what the Cross gave Christ with pain. When He said, "My God, My God, why hast Thou forsaken Me?" He no longer felt His Father's presence, as He had all of His life. Yet even then He trusted. If He had not experienced that "dark night of the soul", that absence of feeling, He would not have shared *all* our desolations and alienations. His test was horribly painful; ours is painless. But it is the same test: what is tested, what is required, is total, absolute, blind faith, faith wholly resting on the object, not the subject; God, not self; fact, not feeling.

This was a hard lesson for a Protestant to learn—this Protestant, anyway. But a precious one. The objective, self-forgetful attitude, at first cold and repelling, I soon found liberating, even Heavenly. For in Heaven we will not have ingrown eyeballs or fondle our feelings or mouth the clichés of pop psychology. We will be in self-transcending ecstasy, stunned and riveted to God. That's why the traditional liturgy is the most Heavenly prayer: it trains us to change self-consciousness into God-consciousness. (See Dietrich von

Hildebrand's *Liturgy and Personality*.) And that's why most modern liturgists are more poisonous than lizards or lawyers.

I thus saw how the very doctrine that seemed at first to repel me could attract me. The same was true of the doctrines about Mary. Like the Eucharist, the Church's Marian doctrines were the last ones I ate and was nourished by. At first, I accepted them simply on the basis of Church authority. The Church says so, so it must be so. (That too, by the way, is a salutary exercise for modern man: to rely on sheer authority, simply to submit, to practice the simple secret of all sanctity, Mary's *fiat*, Mary's unqualified and absolute Yes.) Later, having made the act of blind faith in these doctrines on the grounds of authority without much appreciating them, I did come to appreciate them. Now I see that God *prefers* to work through intermediaries—Mary and the saints—so that He may exalt and glorify them as well as Himself; so He wants us to pray through Mary, and not only directly.

Like most Protestants, I had worried that Mary would divert some love and attention from Christ. This is a very common fear but a very silly one. What else would Mary ever do than to show us the blessed fruit of her womb, Jesus? How could she ever possibly come between us and Christ or bring us farther away from Christ or take Christ farther away from us? Her whole heart and desire and life forever, in Heaven and on earth, is nothing but the ministry of Christ, not of herself. She is the most totally transparent window to Christ, the most submissive one. Therefore the essential Protestant fear, that devotion to Mary might steal honor from Christ, will be answered and refuted precisely by the Catholic Mary. Mary will fulfill all the Protestant's good desires to make sure Christ is all in all.

I embraced the Catholic faith for the only honest reason anyone ever should: because it's true. But I remain a Catholic not only for the abstract reason that I am increasingly certain that it's all *true* but also for the concrete reason that Christ is really present on every Catholic altar, so that to abandon the Catholic Church is literally and concretely to abandon Christ. This helps me understand why so many "dissenting" Catholics stay. Some stay only as spies to subvert the Church, of course, especially some in teaching or administrative power posts. But many stay because of the Eucharist, because they know or believe or hope or suspect or dimly discern that the Lord is there. There is Home. There is the hearth, the fire, the sanctuary lamp. Even when the dissenting Catholic rejects the light, he does not reject the fire. Even when he rejects the truth of some of the Church's teachings, he cannot reject the One who is present there. Such a person is of course very wrong; but he is also very right.

Why be a Catholic? For the same reason a first-century Jew went to the Jerusalem temple in A.D. 30 : to meet Christ, because Christ is there.

This ends my autobiographical testament. Now comes a speculative suggestion about the Eucharist and ecumenism.

I wonder where else He is. How far does the Eucharistic presence extend?

In the Eucharist, Christ is really present but hidden under the appearances of bread and wine. Is He really present in other ways under other appearances too?

The new *Catechism* says He is. Paragraph 1373 says that Christ "is present in many ways to His Church":

1. in His word,
2. in His Church's prayer,
3. in the poor, the sick, and the imprisoned,
4. in the sacraments of which He is the author,
5. in the sacrifice of the Mass,
6. and in the person of the minister.
7. But He is present most *especially in the Eucharistic species.*

It goes on to define this "most especially" in paragraph 1374: "The mode of Christ's presence under the Eucharistic species is unique. . . . The body and blood, together with the soul and divinity, of our Lord Jesus Christ and, therefore, *the whole Christ, is truly, really, and substantially* contained."

This means two things. First, nowhere else is He so fully present on earth as in the Eucharist. But second, He is also present in other ways—lesser but real ways.

Scripture mentions some additional ways. John 1:9 says that the eternal, divine *logos*, the Word of God, the Mind of God, the One who was to become flesh as Jesus, "enlightens every man who comes into the world". So He was present to the mind and conscience of Socrates—and also Alexander. (Socrates seems to have sought Him, and Alexander to have fled from Him.) His presence to pagans is like His presence in the Eucharist in one way: it is invisible and hidden by the appearances rather than revealed.

Where else is He present but hidden?

Might He be present to the dreams of the myth-makers, with their strange stories of dying and rising gods, "as Virgil and the Sibyl say", according to the Church's own "Dies Irae"?

Might He be present in other religions, which, like the myths, are all mixtures of profound truth and profound error? (Except for biblical Judaism, which is also pure divine revelation.) Is there, as Raymond Pannikar supposes, a "hidden Christ of Hinduism"? When a pious Muslim practices his *islam*, his submission, might this be taking place through Christ and His grace and presence, though the Muslim does not know it or acknowledge it?

I think this is very likely. God loves to hide. It is His style. He hides behind His creation. He hides His face from His Chosen People, all except Moses. He hides in Jesus: a carpenter from a hick town who gets crucified as a criminal!

He hides behind the appearances of a little Wafer of bread. He hides in the souls of His people who eat Him when they eat this Wafer. Might He not hide behind many other things? In the souls of Protestants? Vatican II tells us that this is so. In Jews and Muslims? The Church tells us that it can be so. In God-seeking agnostics and pagans? She tells us to hope it is so. She tells us, repeating her Master's words, that all who sincerely seek God find Him. But to find Him is possible only through Christ. Those are the Master's words, too. Therefore Christ must be hiding in these people—which ones and how many, no one knows but God.

This is not an argument for religious indifferentism. We must preach the gospel as passionately as any Fundamentalist who is convinced that he knows that all who are not consciously Christian are on the road to Hell, because we do *not* know who is on the road to Hell. A mother need not know how many of her children will fall through the thin ice and drown before she runs out and screams her gospel of salvation from drowning at the top of her lungs. You need not know when the soul enters the body to oppose all abortions. Precisely because you *don't* know what it is you are killing, you don't kill.

We preach the gospel, not first of all because of what we claim to know about who is saved and who is not, but because we have been commanded to do so by Christ. It does not depend on theology, it depends on obedience.

How far, then, does the Eucharist send its echoes? I do not know, but I would like to quote a suggestion I find very moving and attractive, a suggestion I think is quite orthodox, though I'm not sure. It comes from Teilhard de Chardin, a controversial thinker who I think has written some dangerous and naïve nonsense, especially in *The Phenomenon of Man* and *The Future of Man*, but also some profound and practical and beautiful sense, especially in *The Divine Milieu*. Cardinal de Lubac, at any rate, and some other Catholic thinkers with impeccably orthodox credentials vouch for the value of much of his thought, at least of this part. I quote it to you for your consideration and reaction as an extension of Eucharistic theology and Eucharistic spirituality.

> As our humanity assimilates the material world, and as the Host assimilates our humanity, the eucharistic transformation goes beyond and completes the transubstantiation of the bread on the altar. Step by step it irresistibly invades the universe. It is the fire that sweeps over the heath; the stroke that vibrates through the bronze. In a secondary and generalised sense, but in a true sense, the sacramental Species are formed by the totality of the world, and the duration of the creation is the time needed for its consecration (*The Divine Milieu* [New York: Harper and Row, 1965], pp. 125–26).

The Eucharist may extend, in a secondary and derivative way, to all *matter*, as Teilhard supposes, but how could it extend to all *religions*? How could it possibly be any kind of a common bond or bridge or meeting point between Catholicism and other religions? How could it be ecumenical, either in the proper sense, between the Catholic Church and other Christian churches, or between Christianity and other world religions? Surely it is a principle of division, since it is so distinctive?

But remember something from the first half of this chapter. I found that this doctrine, which seemed to repel and divide, at the same time attracted and united. The same with Mary: she—who is a point of division between Catholics and Protestants—*she* may bring the churches together again and heal the tears in her Son's visible body on earth, she, the very one who seems to divide Catholics from Protestants. The most distinctive Catholic doctrines, especially those concerning the Eucharist and Mary, may prove to be the most unifying and attracting ones.

How can this be?

Let us first notice the logical principle that beneath all disagreements there must always be an agreement. Two boxers must share the same ring before they can hit each other. Two debaters must share the same topic, the same language, and even some of the same assumptions before they can argue against each other, each trying to show that these common assumptions lead to *his* conclusion rather than to his opponent's conclusion.

And in religion, agreement about the ultimate object of faith is the reason for disagreement about the proximate object.

This means four different things on four different levels: Protestant–Catholic, Christian–Jew, Western theist–Eastern pantheist, and theist–atheist.

1. First, the reason for disagreements between Protestants and Catholics is the common Christ. Protestants are Protestants out of devotion to Christ. They think Christ was a Protestant. They think Christ wants them to be Protestants. They think Christ established a Protestant church. When they discover, as I did, that Christ established a Catholic Church, they become Catholics—out of the same original devotion to Christ. The things Catholics and Protestants share in common is Christ.

When I think how much my Protestant brothers and sisters are missing in not having Christ's Real Presence in the Eucharist; when I kneel before the Eucharist and realize I am as truly in Christ's presence as the apostles were but that my Protestant brothers and sisters don't know that, don't believe that—I at first feel a terrible gap between myself and them. What a tremendous thing they are missing! It is as if Christ paid a visit to Capernaum, and a resident of Capernaum didn't bother to come out of his house to see Him. What a point of division the Eucharist is! One of the two sides is very, very wrong. I said before that if Protestants are right,

Catholics are making the terrible mistake of idolatrously adoring bread and wine as God. But if Catholics are right, Protestants are making the just-as-terrible mistake of refusing to adore Christ where He is and are missing out on the most ontologically real union with Christ that is possible in this life, in Holy Communion.

Yet this thought of the gap, the great difference, between Protestants and Catholics is tempered by a second thought: that it is the very same Christ, the exact same Christ, the real Christ, that we both worship. We Catholics can worship Him more fully than Protestants can because we know that He is really present in the Eucharist; but it is the same Christ. We can worship Him more fully, for it cannot be as full a worship if you do not use all the worship tools He left us. Yet, though they cannot worship Him as fully, they worship *Him*, the very one who is present in the Eucharist. That one, there, under the species of bread and wine, our Catholic Christ—that is the One Protestants worship, though not under those species.

2. The same principle applies to Christians and Jews worshipping the same God with or without knowing Christ. A Jew rejects Christ's divinity *for the same reason a Christian accepts it*: out of submission to God and His will and His revelation. *Because* Christians believe God willed to become incarnate in Christ, they worship Christ. *Because* Jews believe God didn't, they don't. The same God! The very same God we worship in Christ is the God the Jews—and the Muslims—worship.

3. The third step is far less clear to me: Do Hindus and Buddhists and Taoists seek the God we have found, or rather the God who has found us, the God of Abraham, even though they do not know Him as the God of Abraham? Is there a "hidden Christ of Hinduism" and even of Buddhism and Taoism?

If the Holy Spirit had not given Saint Paul the Macedonian vision and Paul had proceeded with his plans to take the gospel East instead of West, into Asia instead of into Greece, and if he and John the Evangelist had reached China, and if John's Gospel had been written in Chinese instead of Greek, would it have begun by asserting that "in the beginning was the Tao, and the Tao was with God and the Tao was God . . . and the Tao became flesh and dwelt among us"? No word in any language is as philosophically profound as these two: the Greek *logos* and the Chinese *tao*. And their similarities are very deep, though each one can mean a dozen different but related things. To translate either of them into English, you need a dozen different words or phrases, depending on the context. Both mean the ultimate truth, ultimate meaning, ultimate reality. So when a theist worships God because He is ultimate truth and ultimate reality, isn't that the same thing the Taoist worships, and the Hindu and the Buddhist, under wrong theological ideas, or confused ones, or none at all? Perhaps.

4. Finally, the honest, truth-seeking agnostic or even atheist who seeks truth as an absolute, who will sacrifice for truth, will sacrifice even happiness for truth, will sacrifice life itself, as Socrates did—does such a person also worship a divine attribute and unknowingly worship God under this divine attribute of truth?

I do not know. I hope so. But if so, what has this to do with the Eucharist? Haven't we strayed far from our topic? No, we have extended it. Let us now trace the extension of the Eucharist back to the Eucharist.

To do so, we first move from Truth as an abstract divine attribute to God Himself. We see Truth *as God*, Truth *in God*; but we see *Truth* in God; we worship God *because He is true*.

Then, we move from God to Christ. Again the move is from the more abstract to the more concrete. We see God *as*

Christ, God *in Christ*; but we see *God* in Christ; we worship Christ *because He is God*.

Finally, we move from Christ to the Eucharist—again, to the even more concrete. We see Christ *as Eucharistic*, Christ *in the Eucharist*; but we see *Christ* in the Eucharist. We worship the Eucharist *because it is Christ*.

You see the connecting thread. It is not in ideas but in intention; not objective, but subjective; not in the understanding head, but in the loving, seeking heart. The God who invented the Eucharist is the God who invented the human heart, and He invented the Eucharist to satisfy that heart. Therefore if one follows his heart's deepest hungers, its deepest loves, and its deepest wisdom, then even if he begins as a truth-seeking atheist or agnostic, he will become religious, then theistic, then Christian, then Catholic, if he follows this road consistently and intelligently enough. The deepest thing sought by all religions and all men is the Christ of the Eucharist. And this Christ has solemnly promised that all who seek Him will find Him. Find Him where? If they seek long and hard enough, with all their hearts and all their heads, then they will find Him *there*, where He is, in the Eucharist.

This ecumenical optimism is a necessary consequence of His own promise. It is not an optimism about how many individuals will in fact follow this road to the end. But it is an optimism about the road itself. Nor is it an optimism about solving the problem of comparative religions by any means other than conversion—for instance, by any theological concepts or ecclesial decrees. Nor is it an attack on theological concepts or ecclesial decrees. And it certainly is not a prediction that we will at some time in the near or far future attain a single religious unity in this world, in this life. The only true unity is a unity in truth, and the model and norm for that unity are in the next life, in Heaven, when all who get there will know the truth by direct experience, by seeing God, the same God, the one and only God. In Heaven we will all be one because we will all know God, the God who established the Catholic Church. In that sense, in Heaven we will all be Catholics!

Of course, this perfect unity will be attained only in Heaven. But it is our model now for earth. We pray: "Thy Kingdom come, Thy will be done *on earth as it is in Heaven.*" That is why we invite all to "come and see", to "taste and see" how good the Lord is: we invite non-Catholics to the Church, not so as to divide, but to unite, as Christ did. He said that He would draw all men to Himself.

And how does He do that? Through the Cross: "If I be lifted up [on the Cross], I will draw all men to myself" (Jn 12:32). The Christ of the Eucharist is the Christ of the Cross, a body broken. We will help Him to draw all men to Himself to the extent that we are broken with Him, broken to our sin and selfishness. The world will acknowledge the Eucharist when Catholics become saints. All good men will acknowledge the Christ of the Eucharist when all who acknowledge the Christ of the Eucharist are good men.

Eucharistic ecumenism depends not on theological subtlety but on saintly simplicity. "Blessed are the pure [that is, the simple] of heart, for they shall see God", they shall understand the mysteries of the faith.

A striking encounter with a Muslim student brought this truth home to me—the truth that the simple-hearted see most clearly and that the Eucharist is, ultimately, a very simple dogma. A thoughtful, pious Muslim student at Boston College was engaged in a friendly discussion with a friend of mine about religious differences. He said to my friend, "Do you Catholics really believe that this man Jesus is the Son of God?" "Yes, we do", my friend replied. "And do you really believe that this Jesus is really present there behind that little thing that looks like a piece of bread?" "Yes, we believe that too", he said. The Muslim looked hesitant, and my friend encouraged him: "Go ahead, say what you really feel. I won't be offended." The Muslim replied, "I don't understand how you can really believe that." "Oh, I know," my friend replied, "it's a great mystery and a scandal to reason." "No, I don't mean that at all", said the Muslim, "I mean something simpler. I mean I wonder whether you really believe that or only say you do." My friend asked him, "Why do you wonder whether we really believe that?" The Muslim hesitated again, then replied: "Because if I really believed that, once I entered a Catholic church, I don't see how I could ever get up off my knees again."

Perhaps in Heaven the most ardent worshippers of the Eucharistic Christ will be the "outsiders", like pious Muslims. Even now, without the Eucharistic Christ, they pray five times each day. And we who have Him and know Him—how about us? How often do we pray?

The power that will reunite the Church and win the world is Eucharistic adoration.

These two things—reuniting the Church and winning the world—are parts of the same package deal, the same providential program: the "ecumenical jihad".

Chapter Nine

What Can I Do?

The end of Chapter 4 gives a short answer to this question. This chapter gives a longer answer. The seven-point program here falls into three categories: attitudes, actions, and prayers.

1. "What can I do?" If you are asking this question, you are already beginning to answer it, for you are not just asking *me* for your marching orders (unless you are very, very foolish), but you are asking God—asking Him how He can use you. So, Step One is simply to make that prayer explicit. Tell God something like the following, in these words or your own:

"Lord, I hereby enlist in Your army for Your work for Your Kingdom on earth. Use me as You will. Do with me whatever You will. I write out a blank check to You. You fill in the amount. You are the Lord and I want You to be *my* Lord. Command what You will, and then give me the strength to obey."

You may want to pray Saint Francis of Assisi's beautiful prayer:

Lord, make me an instrument of Your peace.
Where there is hatred, let me sow love;
Where there is injury, pardon;

Where there is doubt, faith;
Where there is despair, hope;
Where there is darkness, light;
And where there is sadness, joy.
O divine Master, grant that I may seek not so much to
     be consoled as to console;
To be understood, as to understand;
To be loved, as to love.
For it is in giving that we receive;
It is in pardoning that we are pardoned;
And it is in dying that we are born to eternal life.

2. Having enrolled in God's army to fight God's jihad, ask Him to help you next to discern to what battlefield He wants to send you, what role He wants you to play. Then look at the opportunities and obligations that come your way, or that are already in your life, as His answer. Sometimes, His answer may be just to keep doing the things you are now doing—caring for parents, children, or others—with a new motivation and consecration and awareness. Sometimes, He may ask you to do new things. The answer may come from without, from circumstances—a request for help, or hearing or reading about a need—or from within, from the desires and interests of your heart. Once you give your heart to God, He will lead you through the desires of your heart as well as through external circumstances—if your desires line up with His as He has publicly revealed them (in the Bible and the teachings of the Church). He may surprise you, but He will never contradict Himself.

3. Some of the ministries (far from a complete list) in this jihad are:

— pro-life work (the most obvious part of the battlefield), for example, opening your home to unwed mothers

— parish volunteer work

— human services work (with the homeless, the handicapped, the retarded, and the elderly, for example)

— ongoing financial contributions

— running for local political office, especially school boards

— clerical work for these organizations

— writing letters to newspapers and journals

— membership in organizations like Operation Rescue that may land you in jail

— membership in formal, Church-approved organizations like Opus Dei, third orders, or Knights of Columbus

— persistent intercessory prayer

4. Attitudes: If you tend to be harsh, angry, and judgmental, ask God to create a clean heart and a right spirit in you, a gentle and compassionate heart like the Sacred Heart of Jesus. If you tend to be lazy, cowardly, and comfort-mongering, ask God for the same heart: a heart as courageous and adamant in its love as the Sacred Heart of Jesus. Attack your own chief fault, out of love for Him and His work. You can't fight His jihad without courage and resolution, and you can't fight His jihad without compassion and love. Dreamy, lazy, weak-willed warriors can do very little good, and angry, loveless warriors can do great harm. So ask Doctor Jesus for a heart transplant operation. He will give it to you in proportion to your desire for it.

If you tend to give up easily, just remember the shortest and greatest graduation speech ever made, by Winston Churchill: "Never, never, never, never, never, never, never, never, NEVER GIVE UP!" If that's good advice on the secular level, how much better—infinitely better—when eternal souls are at stake!

5. Seek out spiritual friends in other religions. Talk together of your common faith and—respectfully—of your different faiths. Pray for *each other's* clergy and leaders. Exchange visits to each other's religious services. Pray together. If you are all Christians, study the Bible together. The point of this is not a sneaky program to convert non-Catholics, but simply to understand and love each other. If you think that's a dangerous thing to do, your faith must be pretty weak. If you think that's a worthless thing to do, your love must be pretty weak.

It could be done with only two people, or with more. It could be done between Catholics and Eastern Orthodox, who have almost everything in common; or between Catholics and Protestants, who have much in common; or between Catholics and Jews or Muslims, who have at least the same God and Commanding Officer in common. The soldiers in this battle had better get to know and love each other if they're going to fight together.

6. Ask God to give you opportunities to witness to your faith, to open your mouth (and to shut it!) as He wills. If each Christian in the world made only one convert in his entire lifetime, every single person in the world would be a Christian within just two generations. What happened in the first few centuries can happen again.

7. The single most important weapon in this battle is prayer. Some specific suggestions:

a. Every day, for the rest of your life, make prayer the very first thing you do when you wake up and the very last thing you do as you fall asleep. As soon as you wake, turn to God, not to the tasks and worries of the day that come at you like a hive of buzzing bees. Offer yourself to your Commanding Officer for whatever spy mission He sends you on today.

b. Daily private prayer is not optional but absolutely necessary. Schedule *at least* fifteen minutes of private personal prayer every day for the rest of your life. If you do not already do this and you think it is just "a good idea to try it", you will certainly NOT succeed. You must fight to do it. The Devil will use every trick in his book to stop you. You must resolve to put God first, put first things first. A definite, deliberate schedule is the only way you will do it.

c. Reschedule and reprioritize your life to allow at least one or two of the following each day: Mass, Eucharistic adoration, Bible reading, family prayers, the Rosary.

d. Consecrate your life to the Immaculate Heart of Mary. She is the one who will win this war. She is the one (as the Bible says) who triumphs over Satan. She is the one all the early Church Fathers call the "New Eve". (See Genesis 3:15.) She is the "woman clothed with the sun" who will destroy the "dragon" (the Devil). (See Revelation 12.)

e. If there is a Catholic charismatic prayer group nearby, explore it. Many have found remarkable new spiritual power through the "baptism of the Holy Spirit". That's how the apostles were transformed from a confused, frightened bunch of losers to world-winners: through the Holy Spirit.

f. Eucharistic adoration, when persevered in, has incredibly revitalized parishes and individuals.

And remember, "Never, never, never, never, never, never, never, never, NEVER GIVE UP!" applies to prayer too. Read Luke 18:1–8 and then ask yourself: Did Jesus ever lie? If He did not, this passage shows us how we will win the world for Him.

CONCLUSION

This book has tried to wake its readers up to nine truths, one for each chapter, nine truths that are simple and crucially important today but still controversial and not yet universally known.

1. We are at war: a spiritual war, a jihad, not between religions, but between good and evil, between all religions and none (Chapter 1).

2. It is not un-Christian to be polemical and belligerent in this war, since our enemies are "not flesh and blood, but . . . principalities and powers" (Chapter 2).

3. It is even right to have "fanaticism", or infinite passion, in this war (Chapter 3).

4. The war is social as well as religious. Security, family, education, and human life itself are threatened (Chapter 4).

5. In forging wartime "ecumenical" alliances, we are encouraged by the Church to learn from other religions (Chapter 5).

6. Confucius, Buddha, Muhammad, and Moses can all remind us of precious but forgotten treasures in our own religion (Chapter 6).

7. Our Protestant "separated brethren" have a different *theology* but not a different *religion*. "Mere Christianity" is more than a lowest-common-denominator abstraction (Chapter 7).

8. Surprisingly, the distinctively Catholic devotion to the Eucharist (and to Mary) may prove to be the key to victory in ecumenism and in the "culture war" (Chapter 8).

9. Persistent, loving prayer can—*will*—win the world.